THE DEVIL'S DICTIONARY
(NEW MILLENNIA EDITION)

A disturbing byproduct of the Cynical Web Site
www.Cynical.ws

Free Thinkers Media
2360 Corporate Circle · Suite 400
Henderson, NV 89074

Copyright © 2012 by Guy Smith. All rights reserved.

All publication copyrights © 2012 by Free Thinkers Media LLC. No part of this document may be reproduced or transmitted in any form, by any means (electronic, photocopying, recording, or otherwise) without the prior written permission of the publisher, aside from "fair use" provisions. Contact info@FreeThinkersMedia.com.

Copyright © 2014 Guy Smith
All rights reserved.
ISBN: 0983240752
ISBN-13: 978-0-9832407-5-4
LCN: 2014938612

Limit of Liability and Disclaimer of Warranty: The publisher and author/editor have used their best efforts in preparing this book, and the information provided herein is provided "as is." Free Thinkers Media LLC makes no representation or warranties with respect to the accuracy or completeness of the contents of this book and specifically disclaims any implied warranties of merchantability or fitness for any particular purpose and shall in no event be liable for any loss of profit or any other commercial damage, including but not limited to special, incidental, consequential or other damages.

Trademarks: This book identifies product names and services known to be trademarks, registered trademarks, or service marks of their respective holders. They are used throughout this book in an editorial fashion only. In addition, terms suspected of being trademarks, registered trademarks, or service marks have been appropriately capitalized, although Free Thinkers Media LLC cannot attest to the accuracy of this information. Use of a term in this book should not be regarded as affecting the validity of any trademark, registered trademark, or service mark. Free Thinkers Media LLC and the author are not associated with any product or vendor mentioned in this book.

All quotes are as received and we make no warranty about the accuracy of their origins. They also arrived with permission, as "fair use" excerpts or as public domain.

Free Thinkers Media assumes all legal responsibility for this product.

DEDICATION

To all the great cynics, past and present (our cynical pessimism leads us to believe there will be no future cynics given mankind's perpetually self-destructive nature).

FOREWORD IS FOREWARNED

A cynic is a person who upon smelling flowers, looks for a casket.

Such is the nature of good natured cynicism. Irritably enlightened people, whose eyesight has been sharpened through exposure to reality, have sought the humor behind this odd thing we call life. Acerbic wit guides the cynic past the cliffs of disappointment because he is disappointed in advance.

Cynical suspicions abound. The database at the Cynical Web Site (www.Cynical.ws) shows that through perfect vision people find democracy one of the most disappointing notions in the nation. Marriage follows immediately, and given that both institutions are defined by whose vote counts the most, there is little wonder.

These same acerbic seers next find fault with disruptive trivialities such as politics, life, patriotism, optimists and love (the latter two often found vigorously copulating). That lawyers, committees and religion are in the same bracket surprises few, though they being the subject of cynical insight more often than civilization itself is confounding.

The original Devil's Dictionary (from which we plundered) was authored by one of America's more advanced cynics, Ambrose Bierce. That this famed author and warrior disappeared in the Mexican desert shows that no amount of cynicism trumps reality or death.

Careful readers of this book will note that many of the wry remarks from cynical observers are repeated. This is not out of laziness on our part, nor sloppy workmanship, but to assure that you find the most precisely devilish dogma where you most expect it.

Above all else remember this: You can *never* be too cynical. There simply isn't enough time.

A  (AS IN "ACERBIC")

A-Bomb:
noun

1. An invention to end all inventions.

abdicate
verb

1. To give up all hope of having a flat stomach.

abdication
noun

1. An act whereby a sovereign attests to his sense of the high temperature of the throne or the overrated benefits of the job.

abdomen
noun

1. The temple of the god Stomach, in whose worship, with sacrificial rights, all true men engage.

> From women this ancient faith [of the Great God Stomach] commands but a stammering assent. They sometimes minister at the altar in a half-hearted and ineffective way, but true reverence for the one deity that men really adore they know not. If woman had a free hand in the world's marketing the race would become graminivorous.
> — **Ambrose Bierce**

ability
noun

1. The natural equipment for accomplishments that distinguishes able men and women from dead ones.

> I think that God in creating Man somewhat overestimated his ability.
> — Oscar Wilde

abnormal
adjective

1. Different enough to make others uncomfortable with your mere presence.
2. Not conforming to prejudice.

> Everyone seems normal . . . until you get to know them. This includes you.
> — Unknown

> To be abnormal is to be different from the majority and thus to evoke fear and loathing in said majority. To be intelligent among the ignorant, to be polite in New York, or to be Republican in San Francisco.
> — Guy Smith

> In matters of thought and conduct, to be independent is to be abnormal, to be abnormal is to be detested.
> — Ambrose Bierce

aborigines
noun

1. The primitive native people of newly discovered lands who till the soil, but soon only fertilize it.

abrupt
adjective

1. Sudden, without ceremony, like the arrival of a cannon shot and the departure of the soldier whose interests are most affected by it.

abscond
intransitive verb

1. An act of magic involving the disappearance of the property of another. See "taxation".

abstain
verb

1. A weakness, the symptoms of which are the temptation to deny oneself pleasure.
2. When voting, the deliberate choice of remaining useless in a given situation.

> A total abstainer is one who abstains from everything but abstention, and especially from inactivity in the affairs of others.
> — **Ambrose Bierce**

absurdity
noun

1. A belief inconsistent with your personal prejudice.

accident
noun

1. The inevitable failure of human intelligence in the face of natural law. See "physics".
2. A condition in which presence of mind is good, but absence of body is better.

> The most likely way for the world to be destroyed, most experts agree, is by accident. That's where we come in; we're computer professionals. We cause accidents.
> — **Nathaniel Borenstein**

accomplice
noun

1. A person associated with another in a crime, having guilty knowledge and complicity – as an attorney who defends a criminal, knowing him guilty.

> When we ask for advice, we are usually looking for an accomplice.
> — **Marquis de la Grange**

accordion
noun

1. A musical instrument in harmony (accord) with the sentiments of an assassin.

> No one can ever again be taken seriously after having played an accordion in public.
> — **Charles Gilbert**

> A gentleman is a man who can play the accordion but doesn't.
> — **Unknown**

accountability
noun

1. The mother of caution.

accuse
transitive verb

1. To establish another person's guilt, typically as a justification for having wronged that person first.

achievement
noun

1 A measure of accomplishment accompanied by the death of endeavour and the birth of disgust.

acquaintance
noun

1. A person whom we know well enough to borrow from, but not well enough to lend.

acting
verb

1. The art of keeping a large group of people from coughing.

> Acting is the most minor of gifts and not a very high-class way to earn a living. After all, Shirley Temple could do it at the age of four.
> — **Katharine Hepburn**

actor
noun

1. Someone who hates himself so much he has to be someone else.

> God writes a lot of comedy. The trouble is, he's stuck with so many bad actors who don't know how to play funny.
> — **Garrison Keillor**

> Actors are the opposite of people.
> — **Tom Stoppard**

adage
noun

1. Truth served pre-digested for those of weak mental constitution.

> The function of an adage is to provide a mindless and popular justification for virtually any point of view – often of contradictory nature – regarding almost any situation. Adages exist for the sole purpose of propping up the vast majority who are distinctly lacking of functional neurons.
> — **Charles Gilbert**

Adam
noun

1. The original sadomasochist, who having a rib cage wound inflicted upon him to acquire a mate, caused all subsequent generations to self-inflict the wound of marriage.

administration
noun

1. An abstraction in politics designed to divert blame from the elected official.

admiration
noun

1. Polite recognition in another of our own traits.

A recent survey was said to prove that the people we Americans most admire are our politicians and doctors. I don't believe it. They are simply the people we are most afraid of. And with the most reason.

— **Unknown**

admonition
noun

1. Gentle rebuke with the meat-axe of intent.

2. A friendly warning devoid of friendliness.

adore
transitive verb

1. To be blind to the faults in others.

We should not be surprised that adoration, which is a fault causing one to see nothing bad in another, is most often used for the various Gods. It is theorized that this is false adoration and instead a complex expression of fear.

— **Guy Smith**

adult
noun

1. A person who realizes all politicians are childish.

2. A person who has stopped growing at both ends and is now growing in the middle.

If you are young and you drink a great deal it will spoil your health, slow your mind, make you fat – in other words, turn you into an adult.

— **P. J. O'Rourke**

adultery
noun

1. A form of amnesia where one forgets who their mate is.

2. The practice of sleeping in the wrong bed.

3. The application of democracy to love.

adventure
noun

1. Bad planning.

advertising
noun

1. The science of arresting the human intelligence long enough to get money from it.

> The very first law in advertising is to avoid the concrete promise and cultivate the delightfully vague.
> — **Bill Cosby**

> What is the difference between unethical and ethical advertising? Unethical advertising uses falsehoods to deceive the public; ethical advertising uses truth to deceive the public.
> — **Vilhjalmur Stefansson**

> Advertising is a valuable economic factor because it is the cheapest way of selling goods, particularly if the goods are worthless.
> — **Sinclair Lewis**

> Chess is as elaborate a waste of human intelligence as you can find outside an advertising agency.
> — **Raymond Chandler**

> In our factory, we make lipstick. In our advertising, we sell hope.
> — **Charles Revlon**

advice
noun

1. The smallest current coin.

> A good scare is worth more to a man than good advice.
> — **Nadine Gordimer**

> No one wants advice – only corroboration.
> — **John Steinbeck**

Free advice is worth the price.
> — **Robert Half**

When we ask for advice, we are usually looking for an accomplice.
> — **Marquis de la Grange**

Advice is what we ask for when we already know the answer but wish we didn't.
> — **Erica Jong**

Solicited advice is fraught with the danger that the advisee may actually follow said advice.
> — **Charles Gilbert**

Good advice is something a man gives when he is too old to set a bad example.
> — **Francois de La Rochefoucauld**

affliction
noun

1. A process of acclimation that prepares the soul for the next and more bitter world.

age
noun

1. That period in life where we overindulge in those vices we still cherish, and revile those we no longer have the strength to commit.

I think age is a very high price to pay for maturity.
> — **Tom Stoppard**

Don't complain about growing old – many people don't have that privilege.
> — **Earl Warren**

Thirty-five is when you finally get your head together and your body starts falling apart.
> — **Unknown**

It is easier to get older than it is to get wiser.
> — **Unknown**

Middle age is when your broad mind and narrow waist begin to change places.

— **E. Joseph Crossman**

You can live to be a hundred if you give up all the things that make you want to live to be a hundred.

— **Woody Allen**

The really frightening thing about middle age is that you know you'll grow out of it.

— **Doris Day**

agitator
noun

1. A political activist who shakes an apple tree in order to dislodge the worms.

agnostic
noun

1. A person of such supreme confidence that they are unwilling to hedge their bets.
2. An Atheist with commitment issues.
3. The origin of indecision.

ala carte
noun

1. God's wagon.

alcoholism
noun

1. The intermediate stage between socialism and capitalism.

alderman
noun

1. An ingenious criminal who hides his thieving with the preteens of open marauding.

alien
noun

1. An countryman in his or her probationary state.
2. A sentient being from a distant planet, bizarre in appearance, manner, and speech. Indistinguishable from a Californian.

> Illegal aliens have always been a problem in the United States. Ask any Indian.
> — **Robert Orben**

alimony
noun

1. The screwing you get after the screwing you did.
2. The high cost of leaving.

> She cried – and the judge wiped her tears with my checkbook.
> — **Tommy Manville**

alms
noun

1. Absolution of guilt via small change.

alone
adjective

1. A state of social isolation craved by everyone except those who have obtained it.
2. In bad company.

Alzheimers
noun

1. The enjoyment several times of a good thing for the first time.

ambidextrous
adjective

1. A political skill allowing elected officials to pick either your left or your right pocket.
2. A skill acquired by your boss allowing him to operate effectively with either the left or right thumb inserted in his nose.

ambition
noun

1. The last refuge of the failure.
2. The desire to be vilified while alive, and ridiculed once dead.

> Women who seek to be equal with men lack ambition.
> — **Timothy Leary**

> Ambition is a poor excuse for not having sense enough to be lazy.
> — **Charlie McCarthy**

American
noun

1. The ability to make anything bigger, louder and disastrously damaging for the sheer joy of doing so.
2. A subspecies of Homo sapiens that eternally vacillate between anarchy and socialism, providing that at any given moment the majority of their population is unhappy.

> [Americans] don't stand on ceremony. They make no distinction about a man's background, his parentage, his education. They say what they mean, and there is a vivid muscularity about the way they say it. They are always the first to put their hands in their pockets. They press you to visit them in their own home the moment they meet you, and are irrepressibly good-humored, ambitious and brimming with self-confidence in any company. Apart from all that I've got nothing against them.
> — **Tom Stoppard**

In every American there is an air of incorrigible innocence, which seems to conceal a diabolical cunning.
— **A. E. Housman**

Americans will put up with anything provided it doesn't block traffic.
— **Dan Rather**

Americans have different ways of saying things. They say "elevator", we say "lift"...they say "President", we say "stupid psychopathic git"....
— **Alexi Sayle**

The thing that impresses me the most about America is the way parents obey their children.
— **King Edward VIII**

The greatest American superstition was belief in facts.
— **Count Hermann Keyserling**

There's no underestimating the intelligence of the American public.
— **H.L. Mencken**

It is said that Americans have no taste, which explains the lack of American cannibals.
— **Guy Smith**

The genius of you Americans is that you never make clear-cut stupid moves, only complicated stupid moves which make us wonder at the possibility that there may be something to them we are missing.
— **Gamel Abdel Nasser**

It's hard to decide if TV makes morons out of everyone or if it mirrors Americans who really are morons to begin with.
— **Martin Mull**

Americans are benevolently ignorant about Canada, while Canadians are malevolently well informed about the United States.
— **J. Bartlett Brebner**

Nobody ever went broke underestimating the taste of the American public.
— **H. L. Mencken**

An American is a man with two arms and four wheels.
— **A Chinese child**

amnesty
noun

1. The act of forgiving crimes caused by those for whom it would be unprofitable to punish.

anarchism
noun

1. Political theory founded on the observation that since few men are wise enough to rule themselves, even fewer are wise enough to rule others.

anger
noun

1. An innate emotion identified by a person's mouth moving faster than their mind.

> Keep your temper. Do not quarrel with an angry person, but give him a soft answer. It is commanded by the Holy Writ and, furthermore, it makes him madder than anything else you could say.
> — **Unknown**

> Speak when you are angry – and you will make the best speech you'll ever regret.
> — **Laurence J. Peter**

Antichrist
noun

1. Any sitting liberal politician.
2. Someone else's Christ.

antipathy
noun

1. The sentiment inspired by politicians, used car salesmen, television news anchors and polka.

antique
noun

1. Something that has been useless for so long it is still in good condition.

apologize
intransitive verb

1. An act that lays the foundation for future offences.

apostle
noun

1. A Disciple working toward a career in politics.

appeal
transitive verb

1. law: to throw the dice once again.
2. law: to ask one court to hold another in contempt.
3. An urgent request typically made under the duress of just guidance or verdict.

appetite
noun

1. The solution to the question of labor.

applause
noun

1. The echo of a platitude.

architect
noun

1. One who drafts a plan of your house for the purpose of planning a draft of your bank account.

architecture
noun

1. The art of how to waste space.

> In my experience, if you have to keep the lavatory door shut by extending your left leg, it's modern architecture.
>
> — **Nancy Banks Smith**

Most of the public buildings of the United States are of the Ramshackle order, though some of our earlier architects preferred the Ironic.
— **Ambrose Bierce**

ardor
noun

1. The quality of love without the burden of knowledge.

argument
noun

1. A disagreement expressed in words rather than bullets.

It is impossible to defeat an ignorant man in argument.
— **William G. McAdoo**

Don't try to have the last word. You might get it.
— **Robert Heinlein**

In a family argument, if it turns out you are right – apologize at once!
— **Robert Heinlein**

The worst moment in an argument is the moment you realize you are wrong.
— **Unknown**

aristocracy
noun

1. Government by the best of men – fellows with fancy hats, clean shirts, and guilty of education and suspect bank accounts (the term is now obsolete as the political theory has proven self-contradictory).

There are no wise few. Every aristocracy that has ever existed has behaved, in all essential points, exactly like a small mob.
— **G. K. Chesterton**

In Europe, aristocracy is founded upon land. In the United States, it is founded upon real estate.
— **H.L. Mencken**

arithmetic
noun

1. The ability to count to twenty without taking off your shoes.

---

arrest
transitive verb

1. To detain someone for being unusual or abnormal.

> God made the world in six days, an arrested on the seventh.
> — **Ambrose Bierce**

---

arrogance
noun

1. Accepting the fact that you are indeed better than everyone else.

> Nobody can be so amusingly arrogant as a young man who has just discovered an old idea and thinks it is his own.
> — **Sydney J. Harris**

---

art
noun

1. The results of personal talent and creativity that will offend someone.

> What garlic is to salad, insanity is to art.
> — **Unknown**

> No degree of dullness can safeguard a work [of art] against the determination of critics to find it fascinating.
> — **Harold Rosenberg**

> Skill without imagination is craftsmanship and gives us many useful objects such as wickerwork picnic baskets. Imagination without skill gives us modern art.
> — **Tom Stoppard**

> The murals in restaurants are on par with the food in museums.
> — **Peter De Vries**

[Abstract art is] a product of the untalented, sold by the unprincipled to the utterly bewildered.
— **Al Capp**

Art is making something out of nothing and selling it.
— **Frank Zappa**

It is only an auctioneer who can equally and impartially admire all schools of art.
— **Oscar Wilde**

Formerly, painting and sculpture were combined in the same work: the ancients painted their statues. The only present alliance between the two arts is that the modern painter chisels his patrons.
— **Ambrose Bierce**

artlessness
noun

1. Having or displaying no guile, cunning, or deceit. This trait is learned from long ago by women and disposed of shortly after vows. Men outside of politics are incapable of the trait.

asperse
transitive verb

1. To maliciously ascribe to another vicious actions for which one lacks the temptation and opportunity to commit themselves.

assassination
transitive verb

1. An extreme form of censorship.

asylum
noun

1. A place where optimism flourishes.

atheism
noun

1. A non-prophet organization.
2. The belief that no god is required to explain greed, hate, sloth, stupidity or political parties.

atheist

noun

1. An evangelist in the church of agnosticism.
2. The ultimate gambler.
3. A man who has no invisible means of support.

> If there were no God, there would be no Atheists.
> — **G. K. Chesterton**

> The only thing wrong with being an atheist is that there's nobody to talk to during an orgasm. What does an atheist say when she's having an orgasm? *Darwin! Oh, Darwin!?*
> — **Unknown**

> I'm a born-again atheist.
> — **Gore Vidal**

> I'm still an atheist, thank God.
> — **Luis Bunuel**

> A dead atheist is someone who's all dressed up with no place to go.
> — **James Duffecy**

auctioneer

noun

1. A man that proclaims with a gavel that he has picked a pocket with his tongue.

Australia

noun

1. A country of the South Pacific whose industrial and commercial development has been unspeakably retarded by the preference of the inhabitants to enjoy life as opposed to submitting to ambition.

author

noun

1. A fool who, not being content with boring those he lives with, insists on boring future generations.
2. A person who has mastered vocabulary and prose but not story telling.

3. A writer with connections in the publishing industry.

autobiography
noun

1. An obituary in serial form with the last instalment missing.

> Autobiography is an unrivaled vehicle for telling the truth about other people.
> — **Philip Guedalla**

automobile
noun

1. A mechanical device enabling us to get away from where we are to where we are no better off.

> The marvels of modern technology include the development of a soda can which, when discarded, will last forever and a $7,000 car, which, when properly cared for, will rust out in two or three years.
> — **Paul Harwitz**

> Natives who beat drums to drive off evil spirits are objects of scorn to smart Americans who blow horns to break up traffic jams.
> — **Mary Ellen Kelly**

avarice
noun

1. The god of the world's leading religion, whose chief temple is in the holy city of New York.

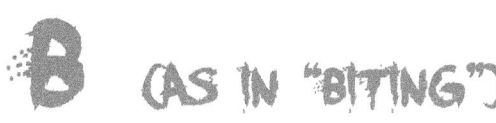# B (AS IN "BITING")

baby
noun

1. A prototype human, incapable of feeling, thought or civil behavior, notable for their ability to generate extreme examples of the same traits in adults.

> A soiled baby, with a neglected nose, cannot be conscientiously regarded as a thing of beauty.
> — **Mark Twain**

> All babies look like homicidal poached eggs.
> — **P.G. Wodehouse**

> The government is like a baby's alimentary canal, with a happy appetite at one end and no responsibility at the other.
> — **Ronald Reagan**

> We all worry about the population explosion, but we don't worry about it at the right time.
> — **Unknown**

> People who say they sleep like a baby usually don't have one.
> — **Leo J. Burke**

Bacchus
noun

1. A god of convenience, invented as an excuse for getting drunk.

back
noun

1. The landing strip for feminine fingernails.
2. That part of the body where the cunning insert the knife, as opposed to the front which is preferred by the guileless.
3. That part of a friend's anatomy that you contemplate during times of adversity.

bacteria
noun

1. The only culture most people develop.

bait
noun

1. A preparation that makes a hook more palatable. Feminine beauty is widely considered the best variety.

balderdash
noun

1. A rapidly receding hairline.

bank
noun

1. A place that will lend you money if you can prove that you don't need it.

A bank is a place where they lend you an umbrella in fair weather and ask for it back when it begins to rain.
— **Robert Lee Frost**

Drive-in banks were established so most of the cars today could see their real owners.
— **E. Joseph Crossman**

Baptism
noun

1. A "get out of Hell free" card.
2. Religious intimidation through drowning.

Traditional Christian ritual require "full submersion" of the Baptismal convert. Reformed sects have selected sprinkling water on the forehead. The former is akin to drowning, and the later a Chinese water torture. In either case, anyone guilty of performing baptisms should be arrested for assault and battery.
— **Guy Smith**

barometer
noun

1. A scientific device to accurately predict what kind of weather we are having.

battle
noun

1. The act of untying a political knot with teeth when it would not yield to the tongue.

> Nobody will ever win the battle of the sexes. There's too much fraternizing with the enemy.
> — **Henry Kissinger**

bear market
noun

1. A period when the kids get no allowance, the wife gets no jewellery, and the husband gets no sex.

beard
noun

1. A modification of age in males that they attempt to grow while too young to deserve the distinction, and which is removed when they are too old to deserve the pleasures of youth.

beauty
noun

1. The power by which a woman charms a lover and terrifies a husband.

> There's a difference between beauty and charm. A beautiful woman is one I notice. A charming woman is one who notices me.
> — **John Erskine**

> Beauty is only a light switch away.
> — **Unknown**

Beauty is in the eye of the beer holder.
— **Unknown**

Beauty is only sin deep.
— **Saki**

A soiled baby, with a neglected nose, cannot be conscientiously regarded as a thing of beauty.
— **Mark Twain**

I think on-stage nudity is disgusting, shameful and damaging to all things American. But if I were 22 with a great body, it would be artistic, tasteful, patriotic and a progressive religious experience.
— **Shelley Winters**

befriend
transitive verb

1. The act of creating an ingrate.

beg
verb

1. To earnestly ask for something in inverse likelihood of receiving it.

beginning
noun

1. The origin of future disaster.

belladonna
noun

1. In Italian, a beautiful lady. In English, a deadly poison. This similarity is widely considered to be proof of the common roots of both languages.

benefactor
noun

1. One who purchases large amounts of ingratitude, yet manages not to affect the price thereof, leaving it affordable by everyone.

beta test
verb

1. To voluntarily entrust one's data, one's livelihood and one's sanity to hardware or software intended to destroy all three. In earlier days, virgins were often selected to beta test volcanoes.

bible
noun

1. Any authoritative book of fact based on fiction.

> When I think of all the harm the Bible has done, I despair of ever writing anything to equal it.
> — **Oscar Wilde**

bigamy
noun

1. Marital gluttony, which carries the heaviest of penalties – multiple wives.
2. Double trouble.

> There is mathematical proof that women are evil.
>
> ```
> Women = Time X Money
> Time  = Money
> ```
> *... thus*
> ```
> Women = Money X Money, or Money²
> ```
> *Now, we all know that Money is the Root of all Evil, so ...*
> ```
> Women = Square root of Evil
> Squared, or SQRT(Evil²)
> Women = Evil
> ```
> — **Unknown**

bigot
noun

1. A small-minded person zealously attached to an opinion that differs from the one to which you zealously adhere.

The mind of a bigot is like the pupil of the eye. The more light you shine on it, the more it will contract.

— **Oliver Wendell Holmes Jr.**

billion
noun

1. A government budgetary rounding error.

A billion here, a billion there, pretty soon it adds up to real money.

— **Senator Everett Dirksen**

birth
noun

1. The beginning of a temporary state. Oddly, this event is widely celebrated.

2. The first, and dirtiest, of all disasters.

Birth to the butterfly looks like death to the caterpillar.

— **Unknown**

As to the nature of [birth] there appears to be no uniformity. Castor and Pollux were born from the egg. Pallas came out of a skull. Galatea was once a block of stone. Peresilis, who wrote in the tenth century, avers that he grew up out of the ground where a priest had spilled holy water. It is known that Arimaxus was derived from a hole in the earth, made by a stroke of lightning. Leucomedon was the son of a cavern in Mount Aetna, and I have myself seen a man come out of a wine cellar.

— **Ambrose Bierce**

body-snatcher
noun

1. A professional who supplies young doctors with the raw material created by old doctors.

2. A person whose occupation is to starve worms.

bore
noun

1. A person who can change the subject back to his topic of conversation faster than you can change it back to yours.
2. A person who opens his mouth and puts his feats in it.
3. A guy with a cocktail glass in one hand, and your lapel in the other.
4. A person who when you ask him how he is, tells you.
5. A person who talks when you wish him to listen.
6. A person who deprives you of solitude without providing you with company.

> The English sent all their bores abroad, and acquired the Empire as a punishment.
> — **Edward Bond**

> It is the dull man who is always sure, and the sure man who is always dull.
> — **H.L. Mencken**

> The penalty for success is to be bored by the people who used to snub you.
> — **Nancy Astor**

> The capacity of human beings to bore one another seems to be vastly greater than that of any other animal.
> — **H.L. Mencken**

> When someone tells you something defies description, you can be pretty sure he's going to have a go at it anyway.
> — **Clyde B. Aster**

boss
noun

1. Someone who is early when you are late and late when you are early.

> When you take a long time, you're slow. When your boss takes a long time, he's thorough.
> — **Unknown**

boundary
noun

1. A divider, real or imagined, designed to enforce civility. See "failure".

2. In political geography, an imaginary line separating the imaginary rights of one people from the imaginary rights of another.

> If "good fences make good neighbors" then I need a new fence.
> — **Guy Smith**

bounty
noun

1. The liberality of one who has much, in permitting one who has nothing to get all that he can.

brain
noun

1. An apparatus for thinking, though this is mere speculation. In the American Republican form of government, the brain is so highly prized that it is rewarded by exemption from holding office.

> Aristotle believed that the brain existed merely to cool blood and was not involved in with thinking, which has proven true for certain persons, mainly politicians.
> — **Derived from Will Cuppy**

> The human brain starts working the moment you are born and never stops until you stand up to speak in public.
> — **George Jessel**

> Men and women both think like spaghetti. Mens' mental spaghetti is uncooked and runs in straight lines. Women's is well boiled and points in every direction simultaneously.
> — **Ralph Seifert**

bride
noun

1. A woman with one child regardless of her current state of chastity or experience giving birth.

2. The female equivalent of a fisherman who has managed to set the hook.

3. A woman whose prospects of happiness are behind her.

broker
noun

1. Poorer than you were last year.

brown nose
noun

1. A useful functionary, not infrequently found editing a newspaper on behalf of a political party.

brute
noun

1. Either of a mean spirited and violent man, or a liquid intoxicant known to create the former.

budget
noun

1. A fiscal system for ensuring that spending reaches a predefined limit even if the organization's income doesn't.

> About the time we think we can make ends meet, somebody moves the ends.
> — **Herbert Hoover**

bull market
noun

1. A random market movement causing an investor to mistake himself for a financial genius.

bureaucracy
noun

1. The engine that keeps the wheels of progress turning ... backwards.

2. The application of order to prevent active chaos, resulting in inactive chaos.

If you're going to sin, sin against God, not the bureaucracy. God will forgive you but the bureaucracy won't.
— **Admiral Hyman Rickover**

We can lick gravity, but sometimes the paperwork is overwhelming.
— **Wernher von Braun**

The only thing that saves us from the bureaucracy is inefficiency. An efficient bureaucracy is the greatest threat to liberty.
— **Eugene McCarthy**

Any sufficiently advanced bureaucracy is indistinguishable from molasses.
— **Unknown**

business
noun

1. The art of extracting money from another person's pocket without resorting to violence.

The music business is a cruel and shallow money trench, a long plastic hallway where thieves and pimps run free, and good men die like dogs. There's also a negative side.
— **Hunter S. Thompson**

He who builds a better mousetrap these days runs into material shortages, patent-infringement suits, work stoppages, collusive bidding, discount discrimination and taxes.
— **H. E. Martz**

I find it rather easy to portray a businessman. Being bland, rather cruel and incompetent comes naturally to me.
— **John Cleese**

No one traveling on a business trip would be missed if he failed to arrive.
— **Thorstein Veblen**

When you looked at the Republicans, you saw the scum off the top of business. When you looked at the Democrats, you saw the scum off the top of politics. Personally, I prefer business. A businessman will steal from you directly instead of getting the IRS to do it for him.
— **P.J. O'Rourke**

Disbelief in magic can force a poor soul into believing in government and business.

— **Tom Robbins**

The gambling known as business looks with austere disfavor upon the business known as gambling.

— **Ambrose Bierce**

cabbage
noun

1. An edible vegetable about as large and wise as the head of a lawyer.

calamity
noun

1. A common reminder that the affairs of life are not of our own ordering.

> Calamities are of two kinds: misfortunes to ourselves, and good fortune to others.
> — **Ambrose Bierce**

California
noun

1. A land of perpetual pubescence, where cultural lag is mistaken for renaissance.

> If they'd lower the taxes and get rid of the smog and clean up the traffic mess, I really believe I'd settle here until the next earthquake.
> — **Groucho Marx**

> California is a tragic country, like Palestine, like every Promised Land.
> — **Christopher Isherwood**

> Whatever starts in California unfortunately has an inclination to spread.
> — **Jimmy Carter**

> Tip the world over on its side and everything loose will land in Los Angeles.
> — **Frank Lloyd Wright**

> California is a fine place to live – if you happen to be an orange.
> — **Fred Allen**

callous
adjective

1. Blessed with the fortitude to tolerate the evils afflicting others.

camel
noun

1. A racehorse designed by a committee.

2. A quadruped useful for crossing deserts, show business, and offending anyone in close proximity.

3. A beast with four legs and two humps – not to be confused with a ménage à trois.

Canada
noun

1. Hell with air conditioning.

2. The vichyssoise of nations: cold, half-French and difficult to stir.

Canada is said to have got its name from the two Spanish words – aca and nada, signifying "there is nothing here."
— **Goldwin Smith**

Very little is known of the Canadian country since it is rarely visited by anyone but the Queen and illiterate sport fishermen.
— **P. J. O'Rourke**

The tragedy of Canada is they could have had British culture, French cooking, and American technology, but instead they got American culture, British cooking, and French technology.
— **Unknown**

The wit of a graduate student is like champagne. Canadian champagne.
— **Robertson Davies**

Canada is like a loft apartment over a really great party!
— **Robin Williams**

cannibal
noun

1. A gastronome of the old school that prefers the simple taste of familiar foods.

> Cannibals are not vegetarians. They are humanitarians.
> **— Unknown**

cannon
noun

1. A device used to certify national borders.

canonical
noun

1. The hats worn by the Jesters of the Court of Heaven.

capitol
noun

1. The seat of misgovernment.

carnivore
noun

1. One addicted to devouring the timid vegetarian and his heirs.

cash flow
noun

1. The movement your money makes as it disappears down the toilet.

cat
noun

1. A pygmy lion who loves mice, hates dogs, and patronizes human beings.
2. A soft and indestructible quadruped adopted by women and used by men as proxy for women during domestic disputes.

I like cats too. Let's exchange recipes.

— **Unknown**

Women and cats will do as they please, and men and dogs should relax and get used to the idea.

— **Robert A. Heinlein**

Cats are to dogs what modern people are to the people we used to have. Cats are slimmer, cleaner, more attractive, disloyal, and lazy. It's easy to understand why the cat has eclipsed the dog as modern America's favorite pet. People like pets to possess the same qualities they do. Cats are irresponsible and recognize no authority, yet are completely dependent on others for their material needs. Cats cannot be made to do anything useful. Cats are mean for the fun of it. In fact, cats possess so many of the same qualities as some people (expensive girlfriends, for instance) that it's often hard to tell the people and the cats apart.

— **P.J. O'Rourke**

Some people say that cats are sneaky, evil, and cruel. True, and they have many other fine qualities as well.

— **Missy Dizick**

Dogs believe they are human. Cats believe they are God.

— **Unknown**

As every cat owner knows, nobody owns a cat.

— **Unknown**

Thousands of years ago, cats were worshipped as gods. Cats have never forgotten this.

— **Unknown**

Cats are like women. If you understand them, they make wonderful companions. If you don't understand them, then they are endless pains in the ass.

— **Guy Smith**

The cat could very well be man's best friend but would never stoop to admitting it.

— **Doug Larson**

Cats are smarter than dogs. You can't get eight cats to pull a sled through snow.

— **Jeff Valdez**

Cats are intended to teach us that not everything in nature has a function.

— Unknown

No matter how much cats fight, there always seems to be plenty of kittens.
— Abraham Lincoln

If cats could talk, they wouldn't.
— Nan Porter

Everything comes to those who wait...except a cat.
— Marilyn Peterson

If a dog jumps in your lap, it is because he is fond of you; but if a cat does the same thing, it is because your lap is warmer.
— Alfred North Whitehead

No matter how hard you try, you can't baptize cats.
— Unknown

Cats seem to go on the principle that it never does any harm to ask for what you want.
— Joseph Wood Krutch

Cats have nine lives, which makes them ideal for experimentation.
— Jimmy Carr

catechism
noun

1. A book giving a brief summary of the basic principles of cats.

A catechism is a formalized, documented, structured review of Christian teachings. This is the ultimate extension of the principle that even the simplest concept can be expounded upon to create perfect misunderstanding.
— Guy Smith

celebrity
noun

1. A person who works hard to become well known, then wears dark glasses to avoid being recognized.

> Today's public figures can no longer write their own speeches or books, and there is some evidence that they can't read them either.
> — Gor Vidal

> A celebrity is one who is known to many persons he is glad he doesn't know.
> — H.L. Mencken

> Some celebrities do well to die young.
> — William Ferraiolo

cemetery
noun

1. The only destination for which you are allowed to run red lights.
2. An isolated suburban area where mourners match lies through inscriptions in stone.

censor
noun

1. A man who knows more than he thinks you ought to.

CEO
noun

1. Chief Embezzlement Officer.

CFO
noun

1. Corporate Fraud Officer.

character
noun

1. What you have left when you've lost everything you can lose.

> People with courage and character always seem sinister to the rest.
> — Hermann Hesse

> A signature always reveals a man's character – and sometimes even his name.
> — Evan Esar

The last time anybody made a list of the top hundred character attributes of New Yorkers, common sense snuck in at number 79.
— **Douglas Adams**

charm
noun

1. The quality in others that causes us to be more satisfied with ourselves.

There's a difference between beauty and charm. A beautiful woman is one I notice. A charming woman is one who notices me.
— **John Erskine**

All charming people have something to conceal, usually their total dependence on the appreciation of others.
— **Cyril Connolly**

chastity
noun

1. An alleged feminine condition resolved with the ample application of jewellery, cash or alcohol.

chicken
noun

1. An animal you eat before they are born and after they are dead.

childhood
noun

1. The period of human life past the idiocy of infancy, once removed from the folly of youth, twice removed from the sin of manhood, and thrice removed from the dementia of old age.

When childhood dies, its corpses are called adults and they enter society, one of the politer names of Hell. That is why we dread children, even if we love them. They show us the state of our decay.
— **Brian Aldiss**

People who get nostalgic about childhood were obviously never children.
— **Bill Watterson**

A happy childhood has spoiled many a promising life.
— **Robertson Davies**

A happy childhood is poor preparation for human contacts.
— **Colette**

Christian
noun

1. One who follows the teachings of Christ in so far as they are not inconsistent with their favorite sins.

2. One who believes that the New Testament is divinely inspired teachings suited for the spiritual uplift of his neighbors.

Scratch the Christian and you find the pagan – spoiled.
— **Israel Zangwill**

Christmas
noun

1. The right holiday celebrated for the wrong reasons.

2. A specific day of the year celebrated by retailers.

Contemporary American children, if they are old enough to grasp the concept of Santa Claus by Thanksgiving, are able to see through it by December 15th.
— **Roy Blount Jr.**

church
noun

1. A building for a weekly devotional and comparison of clothing.

2. A building erected for ecclesiastical fundraising.

If money is the root of all evil, why do churches keep begging for more?
— **Unknown**

People who insist that God is everywhere are usually the same people trying to corral us into churches, mosques and synagogues.
— **William Ferraiolo**

cigarette
noun

1. A device with fire at one end, a fool at the other, and a bit of tobacco in between.

circumcision
noun

1. Premature male lobotomy.

civility
noun

1. The last refuge for the unarmed.

civilization
noun

1. A limitless multiplication of unnecessary necessities.
2. The distance man has placed between himself and his excreta.
3. A societal structure wherein everything is either forbidden or required.
4. The artful form of decadence.

Man – despite his artistic pretensions, his sophistication, and his many accomplishments – owes his existence to a six inch layer of topsoil and the fact that it rains.
— **Unknown**

The first human who hurled an insult instead of a stone was the founder of civilization.
— **Sigmund Freud**

The end of the human race will be that it will eventually die of civilization.
— **Ralph Waldo Emerson**

America is the only country that went from barbarism to decadence without civilization in between.
— Oscar Wilde

It is better for civilization to be going down the drain than to be coming up it.
— Henry Allen

clairvoyant
noun

1. A person who has the power to clearly see what their patron cannot – that their patron is an idiot.

clarinet
noun

1. An instrument of torture, wielded in the most precise fashion by a member of any high school marching band.

clergyman
noun

1. A man who manages our spiritual affairs in order to improve his temporal ones.

client
noun

1. High maintenance customers with low maintenance budgets.

clock
noun

1. A machine designed to rob men of their appreciation of the present through constant reminder of the duties of the future.

college
noun

1. An institution of higher learning where football is taught, though many students major in alcohol.

The theoretical broadening which comes from having many humanities subjects on the campus is offset by the general dopiness of the people who study these things.
— **Richard Phillips Feynman**

Every man should have a college education in order to show him how little the thing is really worth.
— **Elbert Hubbard**

Fathers send their sons to college either because they went to college or because they didn't.
— **L. L. Henderson**

Bachelor's degrees make pretty good placemats if you get 'em laminated.
— **Jeph Jacques**

comfort
noun

1. A state of mind induced by contemplating the distress of others.

commendation
noun

1. A tribute paid for achievements that resemble, but do not equal, our own.

commerce
noun

1. An economic transaction in which A steals from B property actually owned by C, and for compensation, B picks the pockets of D money belonging to E.

committee
noun

1. A body that keeps minutes and wastes hours.
2. An organism with six or more legs and no brain.
3. A group of people who individually can do nothing but as a group decide that nothing can be done.
4. A group of the unwilling, chosen by the unfit, to do the unnecessary.
5. A vehicle with six steering wheels and the engine that has just quit.

If Columbus had an advisory committee he would probably still be at the dock.
— Arthur Goldberg

There is no monument dedicated to the memory of a committee.
— Lester J. Pourciau

Socrates was killed by a committee, so committees are not totally useless.
— John Alejandro King

A committee is a cul-de-sac down which ideas are lured and then quietly strangled.
— Sir Barnett Cocks

To get something done, a committee should consist of no more than three men, two of whom are absent.
— Robert Copeland

A committee can make a decision that is dumber than any of its members.
— David Coblitz

If computers get too powerful, we can organize them into a committee – that will do them in.
— Bradley's Bromide

common sense
noun

1. A collection of prejudices solidified by age eighteen.

> The last time anybody made a list of the top hundred character attributes of New Yorkers, common sense snuck in at number 79.
> — Douglas Adams

commonwealth
noun

1. A governmental entity operated by a multitude of political parasites, inactive and fortuitously inefficient.

communism
noun

1. The worst intersection of a dictatorship and a committee.

Communism is like one big phone company.

— **Lenny Bruce**

Under capitalism, man exploits man. Under communism, it's just the opposite.

— **John Kenneth Galbraith**

complexity
noun

1. The mother of reinvention

compromise
noun

1. An adjustment of conflicting interest in which each party receives the satisfaction of thinking they got more than they deserved, yet are deprived of nothing more than their just due.
2. The art of dividing a cake in such a way that everyone believes he has the biggest piece.

computer
noun

1. An electronic device designed by Satan for the sole purpose of creating pattern baldness through the self-extraction of hair follicles by the user.

A computer lets you make more mistakes faster than any invention in human history – with the possible exceptions of handguns and tequila.

— **Mitch Ratcliffe**

It is easy to be blinded to the essential uselessness of computers by the sense of accomplishment you get from getting them to work at all.

— **Douglas Adams**

A Microsoft Certified Systems Engineer is to computing what a McDonalds Certified Food Specialist is to fine cuisine.

— **Unknown**

The most likely way for the world to be destroyed, most experts agree, is by accident. That's where we come in; we're computer professionals. We cause accidents.
— **Nathaniel Borenstein**

Ours is the age that is proud of machines that think and suspicious of men who try to.
— **H. Mumford Jones**

To err is human – and to blame it on a computer is even more so.
— **Robert Orben**

Making duplicate copies and computer printouts of things no one wanted even one of in the first place is giving America a new sense of purpose.
— **Andy Rooney**

If the automobile had followed the same development cycle as the computer, a Rolls-Royce would today cost $100, get a million miles per gallon, and explode once a year, killing everyone inside.
— **Robert X. Cringely**

Programming today is a race between software engineers striving to build bigger and better idiot-proof programs, and the Universe trying to produce bigger and better idiots. So far, the Universe is winning.
— **Rich Cook**

Imagine if every Thursday your shoes exploded if you tied them the usual way. This happens to us all the time with computers, and nobody thinks of complaining.
— **Jeff Raskin**

In a few seconds a computer can make a mistake so great that it would have taken many men many months to equal it.
— **Unknown**

All programmers are playwrights and all computers are lousy actors.
— **Unknown**

To err is human, but to really foul things up requires a computer.
— **Farmers' Almanac, 1978**

Part of the inhumanity of the computer is that, once it is competently programmed and working smoothly, it is completely honest.
— **Isaac Asimov**

If you put tomfoolery into a computer, nothing comes out of it but tomfoolery. But this tomfoolery, having passed through a very expensive machine, is somehow ennobled and no one dares criticize it.
— **Pierre Gallois**

conceit
noun

1. A disease that makes everyone sick except the person who has it.
2. God's gift to small-minded men and all politicians.

The world tolerates conceit from those who are successful, but not from anybody else.
— **John Blake**

The smaller the mind the greater the conceit.
— **Aesop**

conclusion
noun

1. The point in time when you tire of thinking or writing.

condole
intransitive verb

1. A demonstration that bereavement is a lesser evil than sympathy.

confidante
noun

1. A person entrusted by A with the secrets of B, which were confided to A by C.

confidence
noun

1. The feeling you have before you understand the situation.

All you need in this life is ignorance and confidence, and then success is sure.
— **Mark Twain**

congratulation
noun

1. The civil face of envy.

---

congress
noun

1. The only whorehouse that loses money.
2. A legislative body dedicated to defending liberty, reducing taxes, and improving the general welfare. No historical evidence of such a body exists.

> We may not imagine how our lives could be more frustrating and complex – but Congress can.
> — **Cullen Hightower**

> I might have gone to West Point, but I was too proud to speak to a congressman.
> — **Will Rogers**

> I don't mind what Congress does, as long as they don't do it in the streets and frighten the horses.
> — **Victor Hugo**

> It could probably be shown by facts and figures that there is no distinctly American criminal class except Congress.
> — **Mark Twain**

> This country has come to feel the same when Congress is in session as when the baby gets hold of a hammer.
> — **Will Rogers**

> Suppose you were an idiot and suppose you were a member of Congress. But I repeat myself.
> — **Mark Twain**

> Talk is cheap ... except when Congress speaks.
> — **Unknown**

> In my many years I have come to a conclusion that one useless man is a shame, two is a law firm, and three or more is a congress.
> — **John Adams**

conscience

noun

1. An inner voice that warns us that someone might be looking.
2. What hurts when all your other parts feel so good.
3. What makes a boy tell his parents before his sister can.

> A clear conscience is usually the sign of a bad memory.
> — **Steven Wright**

conservative

noun

1. A person who believes that nothing should be done for the first time.
2. A statesman fond of existing evils.
3. A person with two perfectly good legs who has never learned to walk forward.
4. A liberal that has either been mugged or paid taxes.

> The most radical revolutionary will become a conservative the day after the revolution.
> — **Hannah Arendt**

> The radical of one century is the conservative of the next. The radical invents the views. When he has worn them out the conservative adopts them.
> — **Mark Twain**

> The conventional view serves to protect us from the painful job of thinking.
> — **John Kenneth Galbraith**

consistency

noun

1. The last refuge of the unimaginative.

consolation

noun

1. The knowledge that the winner is likely worse off than yourself.

consul
noun

1. A person who, having failed to secure an office through election, is given one by the administration on the condition that said person leaves the country.

consult
transitive verb

1. To seek the approval of another for a course that has already been decided.

consultant
noun

1. An independent professional who tells you the time, then borrows your watch, tells you the date, keeps the watch, and sends you an invoice equal to the Bolivian national debt.

> Give a man a fish, and you'll feed him for a day. Teach a man to fish, and he'll buy a funny hat. Talk to a hungry man about fish, and you're a consultant.
> — **Scott Adams**

> The only situation in which advice is advisable is in the occupation of consulting. In that situation, give your best advice, take the money, then run like hell.
> — **Charles Gilbert**

contempt
noun

1. A prudent feeling for an enemy who is too formidable to safely oppose.

controversy
noun

1. A battle in which spittle or ink substitutes for ungracious bullets or inconsiderate bayonets.

When a thing ceases to be a subject of controversy, it ceases to be a subject of interest.
— **William Hazlitt**

convent
noun

1. A place of retirement for women of leisure to meditate upon the vice of idleness.

conversation
noun

1. A display of minor mental commodities, each exhibitor being too intent on displaying their own wares to observe those of their neighbors.

Don't knock the weather. If it didn't change once in a while, nine out of ten people couldn't start a conversation.
— **Kin Hubbard**

Most conversations are simply monologues delivered in the presence of witnesses.
— **Margaret Millar**

Saying what we think gives us a wider conversational range than saying what we know.
— **Cullen Hightower**

conversion
noun

1. The act of submitting to religious doctrine, cured by regular church attendance.

conviction
noun

1. The luxury of those sitting on the sidelines.

coronation
noun

1. A ceremony investing a sovereign with the divine right to be assassinated.

corporation
noun

1. An ingenious device for obtaining individual profit without individual responsibility.

> I see the corporate world as a glass neither half empty nor half full, but cracked, leaking, and drowning the staff.
> — **Jerome Alexander**

corpse
noun

1. A pacifist.

coward
noun

1. One, who faced with a perilous situation, thinks with his legs.

> Probably the most distinctive characteristic of the successful politician is selective cowardice.
> — **Richard Harris**

craft
noun

1. A fool's substitute for brains.

creditor
noun

1. One of a tribe of savages dwelling beyond the Financial Straits and feared for their desolating incursions.

criminal
noun

1. A guy no different from the rest, except that he got caught.
2. A person with predatory instincts who has insufficient capital to form a corporation.

3. The chief factor in the progress of the human race.

> It could probably be shown by facts and figures that there is no distinctly American criminal class except Congress.
> — **Mark Twain**

critic

noun

1. A person who boasts that they are hard to please, which is a direct result of the fact that nobody tries to please them.
2. A person who knows the way but can't drive the car.
3. A group of biases held loosely together by a poor sense of taste.

> No degree of dullness can safeguard a work against the determination of critics to find it fascinating.
> — **Harold Rosenberg**

> Asking a working writer what he thinks about critics is like asking a lamppost how it feels about dogs.
> — **Christopher Hampton**

> Pay no attention to what the critics say; there has never been set up a statue in honor of a critic.
> — **Jean Sibelius**

> A "critic" is a man who creates nothing and thereby feels qualified to judge the work of creative men. There is logic in this; he is unbiased – he hates all creative people equally.
> — **Robert Heinlein**

criticism

noun

1. Prejudice made plausible.

cubicle

noun

1. A padded cell without a door.

cynic

noun

1. A disappointed optimist.
2. A well informed optimist.
3. A man who, when he smells flowers, looks around for a coffin.
4. And evangelist in the Church of Reality.
5. A person who is prematurely disappointed in the future.
6. A blackguard whose faulty vision sees things as they are, and not as they ought to be (hence the custom among the Scythians of plucking out a cynic's eye to improve his vision).
7. A pessimistically practical individual, one who believes that the glass is half-empty, and no one is likely to fill it up any time soon.

A cynic is not merely one who reads bitter lessons from the past; he is one who is prematurely disappointed in the future.
— **Sidney J. Harris**

Cynics regarded everybody as equally corrupt. Idealists regarded everybody as equally corrupt, except themselves.
— **Robert Anton Wilson**

No matter how cynical you get, it is impossible to keep up.
— **Lily Tomlin**

cynicism

noun

1. An unpleasant way of saying the truth.
2. The last refuge of an optimist.

Idealism is what precedes experience; cynicism is what follows.
— **David T. Wolf**

The power of accurate observation is commonly called cynicism by those who have not got it.
— **George Bernard Shaw**

Cynicism is a virtue, especially for engineers.
— **David Weinberger**

D (AS IN "DEADPAN")

Damn
verb

1. The 11th commandment, uttered by humans to their Creator, and against their neighbors for only the most minor of infractions.

dance
intransitive verb

1. To leap about to the sound of tittering music, preferably with arms about your neighbor's wife or daughter.

> There are many kinds of dances, but all those requiring the participation of the two sexes have two characteristics in common: they are conspicuously innocent, and genuinely indecent.
> — **Ambrose Bierce**

dancing
noun

1. The vertical expression of a horizontal desire.

> Baptists don't like sex standing up, because it might lead to dancing.
> — **Unknown**

> You should make a point of trying every experience once, excepting incest and folk dancing.
> — **Sir Arnold Bax**

danger
noun

1. A state of imminent personal peril. When the condition is applied to anyone else, it is called "misfortune" or "justice" depending on the level of fondness for the victim.

> It is dangerous to be sincere unless you are also stupid.
> — **George Bernard Shaw**

> It is dangerous to be right when the government is wrong.
> — **Voltaire**

daring
noun

1. The most conspicuous quality of an idiot.

dawn
noun

1. The time when reasonable men go to bed.

> Certain old men prefer to rise at [dawn], taking a cold bath and a long walk with an empty stomach, and otherwise mortifying the flesh. They then point with pride to these practices as the cause of their sturdy health and ripe years; the truth being that they are hearty and old, not because of their habits, but in spite of them. The reason we find only robust persons doing this thing is that it has killed all the others who have tried it.
> — **Ambrose Bierce**

day
noun

1. A period of twenty-four mostly misspent hours.

> [A day] is divided into two parts, the day proper and the night, or day improper – the former devoted to sins of business, the latter consecrated to the other sort. These two kinds of social activity overlap.
> — **Ambrose Bierce**

> I try to take one day at a time, but sometimes several days attack me at once.
> — **Ashleigh Brilliant**

death
noun

1. Life's only certainty.

In the long run we are all dead.

— **John Maynard Keynes**

Life isn't fair. It's just fairer than death, that's all.

— **William Goldman**

Birth to the butterfly looks like death to the caterpillar.

— **Unknown**

The wages of sin is death, but so is the salary of virtue.

— **Unknown**

The wages of sin are death, but by the time taxes are taken out, it's just sort of a tired feeling.

— **Paula Poundstone**

A single death is a tragedy; a million deaths is a statistic.

— **Joseph Stalin**

We seem to believe it is possible to ward off death by following rules of good grooming.

— **Don Delillo**

Life is pleasant. Death is peaceful. It's the transition that's troublesome.

— **Isaac Asimov**

For three days after death hair and fingernails continue to grow but telemarketing calls taper off.

— **Jonny Carson**

Those who welcome death have only tried it from the ears up.

— **Wilson Mizner**

Is there life after birth?

— **Guy Smith**

Amazingly, most people are not ready to die despite having prepared for it their entire lives.

— **Guy Smith**

Death is one of the few things that can be done just as easily lying down.

— **Woody Allen**

What can you say about a society that says that God is dead and Elvis is alive?

— **Irv Kupcinet**

Even very young children need to be informed about dying. Explain the concept of death very carefully to your child. This will make threatening him with it much more effective.

— P. J. O'Rourke

Death is the only goal one can achieve without help, and even then you occasionally receive unwanted assistance.

— Guy Smith

debauchee
noun

1. One who has so earnestly pursued pleasure that he has had the good fortune to achieve it.

debt
noun

1. An ingenious substitute for the chain and whip of the slave driver.

Blessed are the young for they shall inherit the national debt.

— Unknown

Armaments, universal debt, and planned obsolescence – those are the three pillars of Western prosperity.

— Aldous Huxley

decide
intransitive verb

1. To succumb to the preponderance of one set of disasters over another set.

defame
transitive verb

1. To injure the reputation of a person, usually by telling the truth.

defenseless
adjective

1. Unable to attack.

degenerate
adjective

1. To become less conspicuously admirable than your ancestors.

degradation
noun

1. The moral and social journey from private life to political office.

Deja Moo
noun

1. The feeling that you've heard this bull before.

delegation
noun

1. In American politics, an article of merchandise that comes in sets.

deliberation
noun

1. The act of examining one's bread to determine which side it is buttered on.

delusion
noun

1. The father of a family comprising Enthusiasm, Affection, Self-denial, Faith, Hope, Charity, and many other bastards.
2. The natural state of the human mind, set to deny the harsh realities of life and thus suffer them numbly. Greatly enhanced by Hollywood.

> It is a common delusion that you make things better by talking about them.
> **— Dame Rose Macaulay**

> Delusions are often functional. A mother's opinions about her children's beauty, intelligence, goodness, et cetera ad nauseam, keep her from drowning them at birth.
> **— Robert Heinlein**

democracy
noun

1. A device that ensures people will be governed no better than they deserve.
2. The recurrent yet incorrect suspicion that more than half of the people are right more than half the time.
3. Choosing your dictators, after they've told you what you think it is you want to hear.
4. Two wolves and a sheep voting on what to have for dinner.
5. Election by the incompetent many for appointment by the corrupt few.
6. Organized mob rule.
7. The process by which people are free to choose the man who will get the blame.
8. Raising the proletarian to the level of stupidity attained by the bourgeois.

> Television has made dictatorship impossible but democracy unbearable.
> — **Shimon Peres**

> The difference between a democracy and a dictatorship is that in a democracy you vote first and take orders later; in a dictatorship you don't have to waste your time voting.
> — **Charles Bukowski**

> Television is the first truly democratic culture – the first culture available to everybody and entirely governed by what the people want. The most terrifying thing is what people do want.
> — **Clive Barnes**

> Every government is a parliament of whores. The trouble is, in a democracy the whores are us.
> — **P.J. O'Rourke**

> Under democracy one party always devotes its chief energies to trying to prove that the other party is unfit to rule – and both commonly succeed, and are right.
> — **H.L. Mencken**

> The great thing about democracy is that it gives every voter a chance to do something stupid.
> — **Art Spander**

A citizen of America will cross the ocean to fight for democracy, but won't cross the street to vote in a national election.

— Bill Vaughan

Democracy is the worship of jackals by jackasses.

— H.L. Mencken

Democracy is... government by orgy, almost by orgasm.

— H.L. Mencken

Democracy is "representative" in roughly the same sense that the Roman Empire was "Holly".

— William Ferraiolo

In democracy, stupidity always holds the majority in every chamber of government. It is, after all, a representative system.

— William Ferraiolo

Democracy is the name we give the people whenever we need them.

— Marquis de Flers Robert and Arman de Caillavet

As democracy is perfected, the [presidency] represents, more and more closely, the inner soul of the people. We move toward a lofty ideal. On some great and glorious day the plain folks of the land will reach their heart's desire at last, and the White House will be adorned by a downright moron. [Editor: Some people believe this has already occurred]

— H. L. Mencken

dentist
noun

1. A magician who, by putting metal into your mouth, pulls coins out of your pocket.
2. One of the professional class of sadists, the only others of note being the dominatrix and IRS agents (though the different between these two classes is obscure).

dependent
adjective

1. To be reliant upon another person's generosity for your personal support, because you are not in a position to exact such support via fear (ant: taxation).

> To err is dysfunctional, to forgive co-dependent.
> — **Berton Averre**

depression
noun

1. Anger without enthusiasm.

deputy
noun

1. A relative of an office-holder with an intricate system of cobwebs extending from his nose to his desk.

destiny
noun

1. A government's authority for crime and a fool's excuse for failure.

> Lots of folks confuse bad management with destiny.
> — **Kim Hubbard**

diagnosis
noun

1. A physician's forecast of the disease based upon the doctor's detailed examination of the patient's insurance coverage.

diagnostic
noun

1. A person who doubts the existence of two gods.

diaphragm
noun

1. A muscular partition separating disorders of the chest from disorders of the bowels.

diary
noun

1. A daily record of that part of one's life which they can relate to themselves without blushing.

It's the good girls who keep diaries; the bad girls never have the time.
— **Tallulah Bankhead**

Feel free to read anybody's diary. Diaries are not meant to be private. If they were they would be manufactured with a real lock.
— **Guy Smith**

dictator
noun

1. The chief of a nation that prefers the pestilence of despotism to the plague of democracy.

2. A leader elected by the ballot of the bullet, usually unanimously.

Whenever you have an efficient government you have a dictatorship.
— **Harry S Truman**

dictionary
noun

1. A book for making language inelastic. Ignored by Americans.

die
verb

1. The initial phase of fertilization.

Many people would sooner die than think; In fact, they do so.
— **Bertrand Russell**

You live and learn. Or you don't live long.
— **Robert Heinlein**

May you have the good fortune to die on a slow news day.
— **Guy Smith**

> Some celebrities do well to die young.
> — **William Ferraiolo**

> To be willing to die for an idea is to set a rather high price on conjecture.
> — **Anatole France**

> Part of a best friend's job should be to immediately clear your computer history if you die.
> — **Unknown**

digestion
noun

1. The processes of transforming the delectable into the dreadful, unless dining at McDonald's.

diplomacy
noun

1. The art of saying "nice doggie" until you can find a blunt instrument.
2. Lying for one's country.
3. The art of letting someone have your way.

> To kill one person is murder. To kill thousands is foreign policy.
> — **Moh-Tze**

> Take the diplomacy out of war and the thing would fall flat in a week.
> — **Will Rogers**

> In archaeology you uncover the unknown. In diplomacy you cover the known.
> — **Thomas Pickering**

diplomat
noun

1. A person who can tell you to go to hell in such a way that you actually look forward to the trip.
2. A man who always remembers a woman's birthday but never remembers her age.

disabuse
transitive verb

1. To replace an established falsehood with a superior one.

discriminate
intransitive verb

1. To expose elements in a person or thing that are more objectionable than your own.
2. To show preference for one person over another based on inappropriate criteria such as ability, merit, or skill, instead of the socially acceptable differentiations of skin, economic status, or political affiliation.

discussion
noun

1. A method of informing others of their errors.

disobedience
noun

1. The silver lining to the cloud of servitude.
2. The natural state of behavior in children who, through diligent study of their parents, have learned the process of lying.

disobey
transitive verb

1. To celebrate the immaturity of a command.

distance
noun

1. The only thing that the rich give to the poor to call their own and keep.

> The man who says he is willing to meet you halfway is usually a poor judge of distance.
> — **Laurence J. Peter**

> The shortest distance between two points is under construction.
> — **Noelie Altito**

doctor

noun

1. A professional who kills your ills with pills, then kills you with his bills.

If you believe the doctors, nothing is wholesome; if you believe the theologians, nothing is innocent; if you believe the military, nothing is safe.

— **Lord Salisbury**

A recent survey was said to prove that the people we Americans most admire are our politicians and doctors. I don't believe it. They are simply the people we are most afraid of. And with the most reason.

— **Unknown**

dog

noun

1. A pestilent beast kept on domestic premises to insult persons passing by and appall the hardy visitor.
2. A subsidiary deity designed to catch the overflow and surplus of the world's worship. This Divine Being in some of his smaller and silkier incarnations takes, in the affection of women, the place to which there is no human male aspirant.

The average dog is a nicer person than the average person.

— **Andy Rooney**

They say that unless you're the lead dog, the view never changes. Then again, if you're a dog, you probably like that view.

— **John Alejandro King**

I loathe people who keep dogs. They are cowards who haven't got the guts to bite people themselves.

— **August Strindberg**

The virtues we attribute to people at their best – loyalty and devotion, courage and gentleness, integrity and spirit – are found so rarely that we name schools for the men and women who display them. But you'd be hard pressed to find a dog who doesn't live them every day.

— **Scott Raab**

If you pick up a starving dog and make him prosperous, he will not bite you. This is the principle difference between a dog and a man.
— **Mark Twain**

Dogs believe they are human. Cats believe they are God.
— **Unknown**

If a dog jumps in your lap, it is because he is fond of you; but if a cat does the same thing, it is because your lap is warmer.
— **Alfred North Whitehead**

door
noun

1. What a dog is perpetually on the wrong side of.

dot-communism
noun

1. The conviction that everything on the Web should be free or, at least, paid for by someone else.

dragoon
noun

1. A soldier who combines dash and steadiness in so equal measure that he makes his advances on foot and his retreats on horseback.

drama
noun

1. Life with the dull bits cut out.

duel
noun

1. A formal ceremony preceding the reconciliation of two enemies. Great skill is necessary for its satisfactory observance.

I thoroughly disapprove of duels. If a man should challenge me, I would take him kindly and forgivingly by the hand and lead him to a quiet place and kill him.
— **Mark Twain**

One would have thought litigation superior to dueling for the purpose of settling disputes – provided that one had not met a lawyer.
— **William Ferraiolo**

dullard
noun

1. A member of the reigning zoological dynasty with the nasty ability to vote.

The Dullards came in with Adam, and being both numerous and sturdy have overrun the habitable world. The secret of their power is their insensibility to blows; tickle them with a bludgeon and they laugh with a platitude. In the turbulent times of the Crusades they withdrew thence and gradually overspread all Europe, occupying most of the high places in politics, art, literature, science and theology. Since a detachment of Dullards came over with the Pilgrims in the Mayflower and made a favorable report of the country, their increase by birth, immigration, and conversion has been rapid and steady. According to the most trustworthy statistics the number of adult Dullards in the United States is but little more than 300 million, including the statisticians.
— **Ambrose Bierce (updated by the Editor)**

duty
noun

1. That which guides us in the direction of profit, along the line of desire.
2. What should be done without asking, but never is.
3. What no-one else will do at the moment.

When a stupid man is doing something he is ashamed of, he always declares that it is his duty.
— **George Bernard Shaw**

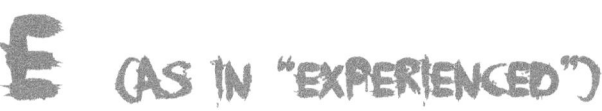 (AS IN "EXPERIENCED")

earnestness
noun

1. Stupidity sent to college.

eat
intransitive verb

1. To perform the functions of mastication and deglutition.

> Eat, drink and be merry – tomorrow you may be in Utah.
> — **On a shot glass in the Salt Lake City airport**

> Eat a live toad the first thing in the morning and nothing worse will happen to you the rest of the day.
> — **Unknown**

> Cockroaches and socialites are the only things that can stay up all night and eat anything.
> — **Herb Caen**

> Man is the only animal that can remain on friendly terms with the victims he intends to eat until he eats them.
> — **Samuel Butler**

eavesdrop
intransitive verb

1. To secretly overhear a catalog of crimes and vices of another, or if unfortunate, yourself.

EBIT
noun

1. Earnings Before Irregularities and Tampering.

EBITDA
noun

1. Earnings Before I Tricked Dumb Auditor.

eccentric
adjective

1. A state of insanity enjoyed by the wealthy.

eccentricity
noun

1. A method of distinction so cheap that fools employ it to accentuate their incapacity.

economist
noun

1. An expert who will know tomorrow why the things he predicted yesterday didn't happen today.
2. A person who states the obvious in terms of the incomprehensible.

> In all recorded history there has not been one economist who has had to worry about where the next meal would come from.
> — **Peter Drucker**

> If all economists were laid end to end, they would not reach a conclusion.
> — **George Bernard Shaw**

economy
noun

1. The aggregate of all theft within a country (hence the larger the government, the greater the economy).
2. Purchasing the barrel of whiskey that you do not need for the price of the cow that you cannot afford.

> People want economy and they will pay any price to get it.
> — **Lee Iacocca**

> The entire economy of the Western world is built on things that cause cancer.
> — **From the movie "Bliss"**

edible
adjective

1. Good to eat, and wholesome to digest, as a worm to a toad, a toad to a snake, a snake to a pig, a pig to a man, and a man to a worm.

editor
noun

1. A cog in the literary machinery responsible for transforming slavish, purple prose into completely unreadable dreck.
2. A person employed by a newspaper, whose business it is to separate the wheat from the chaff, and to see that the chaff is printed.
3. A person who combines the mental clarity of an Alzheimer patient, judgment skills of a crack whore, and linguistic acumen of an immigrant.

> Some editors are failed writers, but so are most writers.
> — **T. S. Eliot**

education
noun

1. State-controlled manufactory of echoes.
2. That which discloses to the wise and disguises from the foolish their lack of understanding.
3. The progressive discovery of your ignorance.

> America believes in education: the average professor earns more money in a year than a professional athlete earns in a whole week.
> — **Evan Esar**

> Men are born ignorant, not stupid; they are made stupid by education.
> — **Bertrand Russell**

> Every man should have a college education in order to show him how little the thing is really worth.
> — **Elbert Hubbard**

> Strange as it seems, no amount of learning can cure stupidity, and formal education positively fortifies it.
> — **Stephen Vizinczey**

> Education is a method whereby one acquires a higher grade of prejudices.
> — **Laurence J. Peter**

> I prefer the company of peasants because they have not been educated sufficiently to reason incorrectly.
> — **Michel de Montaigne**

> The tendency of abstract thought ... is one of the real dangers of the highest education.
> — **Mark Pattison**

> The advantage of a classical education is that it enables you to despise the wealth that it prevents you from achieving.
> — **Russell Green**

> We provide higher education to the masses in much the same way that one might provide a ladder to a jellyfish.
> — **William Ferraiolo**

> A fool's brain digests philosophy into folly, science into superstition, and art into pedantry. Hence University education.
> — **George Bernard Shaw**

effect
noun

1. The second of two phenomena which always occur together in the same order. The first, called a Cause, is said to generate the other – which is no more sensible than it would be for one who has never seen a dog except in the pursuit of a rabbit to declare the rabbit the cause of a dog.
2. The undesired consequence of any carefully planned action.

ego
noun

1. That part of the human psyche responsible for self-preservation and self-aggrandizing, which are natural enemies (often cited by philosophers and other unemployed persons as the source of schizophrenia.)

> When a man is wrapped up in himself, he makes a pretty small package.
> — **John Ruskin**

Egotism
noun

1. An anesthetic that dulls the pain of stupidity.

egotist
noun

1. Someone who is usually me-deep in conversation.
2. The tiny minority of individuals that don't talk about other people.

> The nice thing about egotists is that they don't talk about other people.
> — **Lucille S. Harper**

ejection
noun

1. An approved remedy for the disease of talkativeness.

elector
noun

1. One who enjoys the sacred privilege of voting for their personal preference in pickpockets.

electricity
noun

1. The power that causes all natural phenomena not known to be caused by something else.
2. The seed technology for all forms of modern suffering including unsolicited email, advertising, and television.

elephant
noun

1. A mouse built to government specifications.

elitist
noun

1. Inbred intellectual hemophiliacs who bleed to death as soon as they are nicked by the real world.

eloquence
noun

1. The art of orally persuading fools that white is the color that it appears to be. It includes the gift of making any color appear white.

> The prime purpose of eloquence is to keep other people from talking.
> — **Louis Vermeil**

emancipation
noun

1. A change from the tyranny of another to the despotism of oneself.

embalm
intransitive verb

1. To cheat vegetation by confining the gases upon which it feeds.

> By embalming their dead and thereby deranging the natural balance between animal and vegetable life, the Egyptians made their once fertile and populous country barren and incapable of supporting more than a meager crew. The modern burial casket is a step in the same direction, and many a dead man who ought now to be ornamenting his neighbor's lawn as a tree, or enriching his table as a bunch of radishes, is doomed to a long inutility. We shall get him after a while if we are spared, but in the meantime the violet and rose are languishing for a nibble at his gluteus maximus.
> — **Ambrose Bierce**

emotion
noun

1. A prostrating disease caused by a determination of the heart over the head. It is sometimes accompanied by a copious discharge of hydrated chloride of sodium from the eyes.

> A man's heart is like a sponge, just soaked with emotion and sentiment of which he can squeeze a little bit out for every pretty woman.
> — **Helen Rowland**

end user
noun

1. An irritating noise on a tech support line.

verb

2. A command, regrettably, not implemented in most computer systems.

entertainment
noun

1. Any form of amusement whose inroads stop short of death.

> Boxing is just show business with blood.
> — **Frank Bruno**

> Television enables you to be entertained in your home by people you wouldn't have in your home.
> — **David Frost**

> One of the few good things about modern times: If you die horribly on television, you will not have died in vain. You will have entertained us.
> — **Kurt Vonnegut**

enthusiasm
noun

1. A distemper of youth, curable by small doses of repentance in connection with experience.

envelope
noun

1. The coffin of a document; the scabbard of a bill; the husk of a remittance; the bed-gown of a love-letter.

envy
noun

1. Emulation adapted to the meanest usage.

epaulet
noun

1. An ornamented badge, serving to distinguish a military officer from the enemy – namely the officer of lower rank to whom his death would give promotion.

epitaph
noun

1. An inscription on a tomb, showing that virtues acquired after death have a retroactive effect.

erudition
noun

1. Dust shaken out of a book into an empty skull.

esoteric
adjective

1. Philosophy that is particularly abstruse and consummately occult.

et cetera
noun

1. A word to make others believe that you know more than you actually do.
2. Blah, blah, blah.

ethnology
noun

1. The art of robbing the humanity from humanity.
2. The science that treats the various tribes of Man, as robbers, thieves, swindlers, dunces, lunatics, idiots, and ethnologists.

eucharist
noun

1. Cannibalism as practiced by Christians.
2. The first act of religious conversion through missionary work with native cannibals.

eulogy
noun

1. Praise of a person who has either the advantages of wealth and power, or the consideration to be dead.

evangelist
noun

1. A bearer of good religious tidings, particularly in assuring us of our own salvation and the damnation of our neighbors.
2. Anyone that zealously promotes their beliefs well past the point of annoyance.

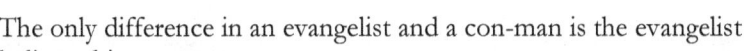

> The only difference in an evangelist and a con-man is the evangelist believes his own con.
> — **Mark Twain**

evil
noun

1. Your opponent's moral philosophy.

> If money is the root of all evil, why do churches keep begging for more?
> — **Unknown**

Knowledge is power, but power corrupts. So study hard and be evil.

— **Unknown**

The fundamental evil of the world arose from the fact that the good Lord has not created money enough.

— **Heinrich Heine**

If you believe there is good in everybody, then you haven't met everybody.

— **Unknown**

Men never do evil so completely and cheerfully as when they do it from a religious conviction.

— **Blaise Pascal**

With or without religion, you would have good people doing good things and evil people doing evil things. But for good people to do evil things, that takes religion.

— **Steven Weinberg**

I believe that all government is evil, and that trying to improve it is largely a waste of time.

— **H.L. Mencken**

Whenever I'm caught between two evils, I take the one I've never tried.

— **Mae West**

Self-deception is the root of all evil.

— **Unknown**

exception
noun

1. Anything which takes the liberty to differ from other things of its class, such as an honest man or a truthful woman.

"The exception proves the rule" is an expression constantly upon the lips of the ignorant, who parrot it from one another with never a thought of its absurdity. In the Latin, "Exceptio probat regulam" means that the exception tests the rule, puts it to the proof, not confirm it. The malefactor who drew the meaning from this excellent dictum and substituted a contrary one of his own exerted an evil power which appears to be immortal.

— **Ambrose Bierce**

excess
noun

1. An indulgence beyond the reasonable limits of moderation defined by your neighbors.

> Excess on occasion is exhilarating. It prevents moderation from acquiring the deadening effect of a habit.
> — **W. Somerset Maugham**

excommunication
noun

1. The involuntary expulsion of a heathen from an organization noted for holy wars and human sacrifices.

executioner
noun

1. An officer of the law charged with duties of the utmost gravity, and held in disesteem by a populace having a criminal ancestry.

> In some of the American States his functions are now performed by an electrician, as in New Jersey, where executions by electricity have recently been ordered – the first instance known to this lexicographer of anybody questioning the expediency of hanging Jerseymen.
> — **Ambrose Bierce**

executive
noun

1. government: an officer whose duty it is to enforce the wishes of the people through legislative power until such time as the judicial branch pronounces them [the people] invalid and of no effect.
2. business: the highest ranks of mismanagement.

> Dealing with network executives is like being nibbled to death by ducks.
> — **Eric Sevareid**

exhort
transitive verb

1. In religious affairs, to put the conscience of another upon the spit and roast it to a nut-brown discomfort.

exile
noun

1. One who serves his country by residing abroad.

expatriate
noun

1. A person of intelligence who realizes that love of country is always trumped by retention of wealth or preservation of hide.
2. A person with income who has the forethought to avoid taxation.

experience
noun

1. What enables you to recognize a mistake when you make it again.
2. Wisdom that enables us to recognize an undesirable old folly that we have already embraced and warmly remember.

> Human beings, who are almost unique in having the ability to learn from the experience of others, are also remarkable for their apparent disinclination to do so.
> — **Douglas Adams**

> Experience is what allows us to repeat our mistakes, only with more finesse!
> — **Derwood Fincher**

> You should make a point of trying every experience once, excepting incest and folk dancing.
> — **Sir Arnold Bax**

> Experience is the name everyone gives to their mistakes.
> — **Oscar Wilde**

Good judgment comes from experience. Experience comes from bad judgment.
— **Unknown**

Experience is the worst teacher; it gives the test before presenting the lesson.
— **Vernon Law**

We spend the first half of our lives gathering experiences that we repeat endlessly in the second half.
— **Guy Smith**

expert
noun

1. A person with more data than judgment.

2. A person knowledgeable enough about what is going on to be scared.

3. A person who avoids small error as he sweeps on to the grand fallacy.

4. A specialist who knows everything about something, and nothing about anything else.

If the world should blow itself up, the last audible voice would be that of an expert saying it can't be done.
— **Peter Ustinov**

Where facts are few, experts are many.
— **Donald R. Gannon**

An expert is a person who has made all the mistakes that can be made in a very narrow field.
— **Niels Bohr**

Always listen to experts. They'll tell you what can't be done and why. Then do it.
— **Robert Heinlein**

expostulation
noun

1. One of the many methods by which fools prefer to lose their friends.

extinction

noun

1. The raw material from which theology created the future state.

> More than any other time in history, mankind faces a crossroads. One path leads to despair and utter hopelessness. The other, to total extinction. Let us pray we have the wisdom to choose correctly.
> — **Woody Allen**

F (AS IN FOLLY)

faith
noun

1. Belief without evidence in what is told by one who speaks without knowledge, of things without parallel.
2. Tactical truth avoidance.

> Faith may be defined briefly as an illogical belief in the occurrence of the improbable.
> — **H. L. Mencken**

> Absolute faith corrupts as absolutely as absolute power.
> — **Eric Hoffer**

famous
adjective

1. Conspicuously miserable.

fanaticism
noun

1. Redoubling of effort once the goal is forgotten.

fashion
noun

1. Something that goes in one year and out the other.
2. A despot whom the populace ridicules and obeys.

> What a man most enjoys about a woman's clothes are his fantasies of how she would look without them.
> — **Brendan Francis**

Women dress alike all over the world: they dress to be annoying to other women.
— **Elsa Schiaparelli**

It's always the badly dressed people who are the most interesting.
— **Jean Paul Gaultier**

A fashion is nothing but an induced epidemic.
— **George Bernard Shaw**

Fashion is a form of ugliness so intolerable that we have to alter it every six months.
— **Oscar Wilde**

father
noun

1. A banker provided by nature.

By the time a man realizes that maybe his father was right, he usually has a son who thinks he's wrong.
— **Charles Wadsworth**

felon
noun

1. A person of greater enterprise than discretion.

female
noun

1. One of the opposing or unfair sex.

fertilizer
noun

1. The final useful purpose of humans.

festival
noun

1. A religious celebration usually signalled by gluttony and drunkenness, frequently in honor of some holy person distinguished for abstemiousness.

feudalism
noun

1. A system of government where your vote does not count, but your count does vote.

fib
noun

1. A habitual liar's nearest approach to truth: the perigee of his eccentric orbit.
2. A lie in the larval state.

fickleness
noun

1. The repeating gluttony of an enterprising affection.

fiddle
noun

1. An instrument to tickle human ears by creating friction between a horse's tail a cat's entrails.

fidelity
noun

1. A virtue peculiar to those who are about to be betrayed.

finance
noun

1. The art or science of managing revenues and resources for the best advantage of the manager.
2. The process of passing money from hand to hand until it finally disappears.

financial planner
noun

1. A guy who actually remembers his wallet when he runs to the 7-11 for toilet paper and cigarettes.

flag

noun

1. A colored rag used to symbolize confederations of convenience.

> There is hopeful symbolism in the fact that flags do not wave in a vacuum.
> — **Arthur C. Clarke**

flashlight

noun

1. A case for holding dead batteries.

flesh

noun

1. The Second Person of the secular Trinity.

flood

noun

1. The original baptism which washed away the sins (and sinners) of the world.

fly-speck

noun

1. The prototype of punctuation.

folly

noun

1. Life.

> One man's folly is another man's wife.
> — **Helen Rowland**

> The most common of all follies is to believe passionately in the palpably not true. It is the chief occupation of mankind.
> — **H. L. Mencken**

fool

noun

1. A person who pervades the domain of intellectual speculation and diffuses himself through the channels of moral activity.

Get all the fools on your side and you can be elected to anything.
— **Frank Dane**

It is better to keep your mouth closed and let people think you are a fool than to open it and remove all doubt.
— **Mark Twain**

Rogues are preferable to imbeciles because they sometimes take a rest.
— **Alexandre Dumas**

The surprising thing about young fools is how many survive to become old fools.
— **Doug Larson**

Any fool can criticize, condemn, and complain – and most fools do.
— **Dale Carnegie**

Fools rush in where fools have been before.
— **Unknown**

A fellow who is always declaring he's no fool usually has his suspicions.
— **Wilson Mizner**

[The fool] is omnific, omniform, omnipercipient, omniscience, omnipotent. He it was who invented letters, printing, the railroad, the steamboat, the telegraph, the platitude and the circle of the sciences. He created patriotism and taught the nations war – founded theology, philosophy, law, medicine and Chicago. He established monarchical and republican government. He is from everlasting to everlasting – such as creation's dawn beheld he fooleth now. In the morning of time he sang upon primitive hills, and in the noonday of existence headed the procession of being. His grandmotherly hand was warmly tucked-in the set sun of civilization, and in the twilight he prepares Man's evening meal of milk-and-morality and turns down the covers of the universal grave. And after the rest of us shall have retired for the night of eternal oblivion he will sit up to write a history of human civilization.
— **Ambrose Bierce**

forefinger
noun

1. The finger commonly used in pointing out two malefactors.

Foreign aid
noun

1. A transfer from poor people in rich countries to rich people in poor countries.

forgetfulness
noun

1. A gift of God bestowed upon people in compensation for their destitution of conscience.

fork
noun

1. An instrument used chiefly for the purpose of putting dead animals into the mouth.

> Formerly the knife was employed for [putting dead animals into our mouths], and by many worthy persons is still thought to have many advantages over the [fork], which, however, they do not altogether reject, but use to assist in charging the knife. The immunity of these persons from swift and awful death is one of the most striking proofs of God's mercy to those that hate Him.
> — **Ambrose Bierce**

freedom
noun

1. Exemption from the stress of authority.
2. A political condition that every nation supposes itself to enjoy in virtual monopoly.

> Ammunition beats persuasion when you're looking for freedom.
> — **Will Rogers**

It is by the goodness of God that in our country we have those three unspeakably precious things: freedom of speech, freedom of conscience, and the prudence never to practice either.
— **Mark Twain**

People demand freedom of speech as a compensation for the freedom of thought which they seldom use.
— **Soren Kierkegaard**

Freedom is just Chaos, with better lighting.
— **Alan Dean Foster**

freemasons
noun

1. An order with secret rites, grotesque ceremonies, and fantastic costumes.

[An order] which, originating in the reign of Charles II, among working artisans of London, has been joined successively by the dead of past centuries in unbroken retrogression until now it embraces all the generations of man on the hither side of Adam and is drumming up distinguished recruits among the pre-Creational inhabitants of Chaos and Formless Void. The order was founded at different times by Charlemagne, Julius Caesar, Cyrus, Solomon, Zoroaster, Confucious, Thothmes, and Buddha. Its emblems and symbols have been found in the Catacombs of Paris and Rome, on the stones of the Parthenon and the Chinese Great Wall, among the temples of Karnak and Palmyra and in the Egyptian Pyramids – always by a Freemason.
— **Ambrose Bierce**

friend
noun

1. A disease incurred by exposure to prosperity.
2. An acquaintance who has not screwed you ... yet.

Nothing changes your opinion of a friend so surely as success – yours or his.
— **Franklin P. Jones**

A good friend will come and bail you out of jail. A true friend will be sitting next to you in the cell saying "Damn, that was fun!"

— Unknown

A true friend will stab you in the front.

— Oscar Wilde

Friends may come and go, but enemies accumulate.

— Thomas Jones

Money can't buy friends, but it can get you a better class of enemy.

— Spike Milligan

It is easier to forgive an enemy than to forgive a friend.

— William Blake

A friend is someone who will help you move. A real friend is someone who will help you move a body.

— Unknown

You never know exactly how many friends you have until you own a house at the beach.

— Unknown

A friend in need is a pest in deed.

— Anonymous

friendless
adjective

1. Addicted to utterance of truth and common sense.

2. Having no favors to bestow.

friendship
noun

1. A ship big enough to carry two in fair weather, but only one in foul.

frog
noun

1. A reptile with edible legs.

2. A diligent songster, having a good voice but no ear.

frying pan
noun

1. One part of the penal apparatus employed in that punitive institution, a woman's kitchen.

funeral
noun

1. A pageant where we prove our respect for the dead by enriching the undertaker, and increase our grief through the same expense.

> No matter how rich you become, how famous or powerful, when you die the size of your funeral will still pretty much depend on the weather.
> **— Michael Pritchard**

> The only difference between a wedding and a funeral is there is one less person standing at a funeral.
> **— Cliff Cole**

future
noun

1. That period of time (which never arrives) in which our affairs prosper, our friends are true, and our happiness is assured.

> To live in the past or in the future may be less satisfying than to live in the present, but it can never be as disillusioning.
> **— R. D. Laing**

> The future, according to some scientists, will be exactly like the past, only far more expensive.
> **— John Sladek**

> The future is here. It's just not widely distributed yet.
> **— William Gibson**

> I have seen the future and it doesn't work.
> **— Robert Fulford**

> The future is not what it used to be.
> **— Paul Valery**

G 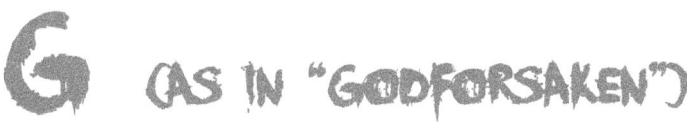 (AS IN "GODFORSAKEN")

gallows
noun

1. A stage for the performance of miracle plays, in which the leading actor is translated to heaven.

> In this country the gallows is chiefly remarkable for the number of persons who escape it.
> — **Ambrose Bierce**

gargoyle
noun

1. A rainspout projecting from the eaves of medieval buildings, commonly fashioned into a grotesque caricature of some personal enemy of the architect or owner of the building.

garter
noun

1. An elastic band intended to keep a woman from coming out of her stockings and make men attempt the feat.

genealogy
noun

1. An account of one's descent from an ancestor who did not particularly care to trace his own.

generous
adjective

1. A personality trait responsible for our abundance of ingratitude and "victimization".

Originally [generous] meant noble by birth and was rightly applied to a great multitude of persons. It now means noble by nature and is taking a bit of a rest.

— **Ambrose Bierce**

gentleman
noun

1. A man who can play the accordion but doesn't.

geographer
noun

1. A person who can tell you the difference between the outside of the world and the inside.

geography
noun

1. The mapping of the divisions of the earth resulting from either the whims of God or the imbecility of man.

God's [geography] deals with physical boundaries (oceans, mountains, etc.) while man's deals with arbitrary boundaries composed of the currently popular state of ill will and suspicion.

— **Ambrose Bierce**

geology
noun

1. The study of the earth's crust, as opposed to humanism, the study of the parasitic infestation of the earth's crust.
2. A study of the composition of the earth we conduct the morning after the earthquake.

The geological formations of the globe already noted are catalogued thus: The Primary, or lower one, consists of rocks, bones or mired mules, gas-pipes, miners' tools, antique statues minus the nose, Spanish doubloons and ancestors. The Secondary is largely made up of red worms and moles. The Tertiary comprises railway tracks, patent pavements, grass, snakes, moldy boots, beer bottles, tomato cans, intoxicated citizens, garbage, anarchists, snap-dogs and fools.

— **Ambrose Bierce**

ghost
noun

1. The outward and visible sign of an inward fear.

There is one insuperable obstacle to a belief in ghosts. A ghost never comes naked: he appears either in a winding-sheet or "in his habit as he lived." To believe in him, then, is to believe that not only have the dead the power to make themselves visible after there is nothing left of them, but that the same power inheres in textile fabrics.

— **Ambrose Bierce**

ghoul
noun

1. A post-modern cannibal.
2. A demon addicted to the reprehensible habit of devouring the dead. Contrast with a tax collector, who has the reprehensible habit of devouring the living.

The existence of ghouls has been disputed by that class of controversialists who are more concerned to deprive the world of comforting beliefs than to give it anything good in their place.

As late as the beginning of the fourteenth century a ghoul was cornered in the crypt of the cathedral at Amiens and the whole population surrounded the place. Twenty armed men with a priest at their head, bearing a crucifix, entered and captured the ghoul, which, thinking to escape by the stratagem, had transformed itself to the semblance of a well-known citizen, but was nevertheless hanged, drawn and quartered in the midst of hideous popular orgies. The citizen whose shape the demon had assumed was so affected by the sinister occurrence that he never again showed himself in Amiens and his fate remains a mystery.

— **Ambrose Bierce**

glutton
noun

1. A person who escapes the evils of moderation.

---

god
noun

1. A superior being cursed with all the petty frailties of man, and upon whom we can thus lay blame for all woes.

One man's God often is another man's abomination.
— **Unknown**

It says he made us all to be just like him. So if we're dumb, then God is dumb, and maybe even a little ugly on the side.
— **Frank Zappa**

If God created us in His own image, we have more than reciprocated.
— **Unknown**

You know your god is man-made when he hates all the same people you do.
— **Unknown**

Everyone is as God has made him, and oftentimes a great deal worse.
— **Miguel de Cervantes**

God, please save us from your followers.
— **Unknown**

Religion fails from the start, by trying to conceive of God, who by definition is inconceivable.
— **Guy Smith**

God writes a lot of comedy. The trouble is he's stuck with so many bad actors who don't know how to play funny.
— **Garrison Keillor**

Would a kind, just and merciful God allow lawyers to live?
— **Guy Smith**

When the gods wish to punish us, they answer our prayers.
— **Oscar Wilde**

If you're going to sin, sin against God, not the bureaucracy. God will forgive you but the bureaucracy won't.

— **Admiral Hyman Rickover**

According to theology, in the beginning there was void and from the void, God created the universe. According to scientists, in the beginning there was void, and from the void the universe created itself. Looks like God is up by one point at half time.

— **Guy Smith**

God is a comedian playing to an audience too afraid to laugh.

— **Voltaire**

They say the reason we can't see God is that God is everywhere. Which makes sense . . . I can't see THEM either, but they're everywhere too. Let's hope THEY aren't God.

— **John Alejandro King**

They say that God is everywhere, and yet we always think of Him as somewhat of a recluse.

— **Emily Dickinson**

To you I'm an atheist; to God, I'm the Loyal Opposition.

— **Woody Allen**

The gods too are fond of a joke.

— **Aristotle**

I'm still an atheist, thank God.

— **Luis Bunuel**

I think that God in creating Man somewhat overestimated his ability.

— **Oscar Wilde**

Dogs believe they are human. Cats believe they are God.

— **Unknown**

God is not dead but alive and well and working on a much less ambitious project.

— **Unknown**

What can you say about a society that says that God is dead and Elvis is alive?

— **Irv Kupcinet**

Nobody talks so constantly about God as those who insist that there is no God.

— **Heywood Broun**

God invented sex and we give praise to him at every orgasm by shouting "Oh, my God."
— **Guy Smith**

An honest God is the noblest work of man.
— **Robert G. Ingersoll**

If a man says that he fears God, do not ask for a demonstration.
— **William Ferraiolo**

People who insist that God is everywhere are usually the same people trying to corral us into churches, mosques and synagogues.
— **William Ferraiolo**

I don't know if God exists, but it would be better for His reputation if He didn't.
— **Jules Renard**

And God said "Let there be Satan, so people don't blame everything on me. And let there be lawyers, so people don't blame everything on Satan."
— **Unknown**

God is love, I dare say. But what a mischievous devil love is.
— **Samuel Butler**

Power corrupts, absolute power corrupts absolutely. What does this say about God?
— **Guy Smith**

golf
noun

1. Nature's way of telling you that you should be dead.

Long ago when men cursed and beat the ground with sticks, it was called witchcraft. Today it's called golf.
— **Will Rogers**

Although golf was originally restricted to wealthy, overweight Protestants, today it's open to anybody who owns hideous clothing.
— **Dave Barry**

Golf and sex are about the only things you can enjoy without being good at.

— Jimmy Demaret

If you watch a game, it's fun. If you play at it, it's recreation. If you work at it, it's golf.

— Bob Hope

The income tax has made liars out of more Americans than golf.

— Will Rogers

good
adjective

1. Of marginally superior quality, as in "a morally repugnant politician".

The good people sleep much better at night than the bad people. Of course, the bad people enjoy the waking hours much more.

— Woody Allen

In the United States, doing good has come to be, like patriotism, a favorite device of persons with something to sell.

— H.L. Mencken

On the whole human beings want to be good, but not too good and not quite all the time.

— George Orwell

If you believe there is good in everybody, then you haven't met everybody.

— Unknown

Beware beautiful women, charismatic men, and all mention of "common good".

— William Ferraiolo

Being a "good citizen" is largely a matter of emulating the least interesting members of one's society.

— William Ferraiolo

goose
noun

1. A wild bird often found landing in the southern perimeter of young ladies.

gossip
noun

1. A person who will never tell a lie if the truth will do more damage.
2. What is said about objects of flattery when they are not present.

The only time people dislike gossip is when you gossip about them.
— **Will Rogers**

No one gossips about other people's secret virtues.
— **Bertrand Russell**

You never see a fish on the wall with its mouth shut.
— **Unknown**

gout
noun

1. A physician's name for the rheumatism of a rich patient.

government
noun

1. A system of rule through which everybody endeavors to live at the expense of everybody else.

Trickery is what humans are all about ... They're so keen on tricking one another all the time that elect governments to do it for them.
— **Terry Pratchett**

It doesn't matter who you vote for ... the government always gets in.
— **Unknown**

Whenever the Government denies knowledge, it is always speaking the truth.
— **John Alejandro King**

The government is like a baby's alimentary canal, with a happy appetite at one end and no responsibility at the other.
— **Ronald Reagan**

Thank God we don't get all the government we pay for.
— **Will Rogers**

Nothing is so permanent as a temporary government program.

— **Milton Friedman**

Every government is a parliament of whores. The trouble is, in a democracy the whores are us.

— **P.J. O'Rourke**

Government is morally wrong. The whole idea of our government is this: If enough people get together and act in concert, they can take something and not pay for it.

— **P.J. O'Rourke**

Feeling good about government is like looking on the bright side of any catastrophe. When you quit looking, the catastrophe is still there.

— **P.J. O'Rourke**

It is a popular delusion that the government wastes vast amounts of money through inefficiency and sloth. Enormous effort and elaborate planning are required to waste this much money.

— **P.J. O'Rourke**

A little government and a little luck are necessary in life, but only a fool trusts either of them.

— **P.J. O'Rourke**

Washington is a place where people praise courage and act on elaborate personal cost-benefit calculations.

— **John Kenneth Galbraith**

Giving money and power to government is like giving whiskey and car keys to teenage boys.

— **P.J. O'Rourke**

Whenever you have an efficient government you have a dictatorship.

— **Harry S Truman**

The government consists of a gang of men exactly like you and me. They have, taking one with another, no special talent for the business of government; they have only a talent for getting and holding office.

— **H.L. Mencken**

There is no nonsense so errant that it cannot be made the creed of the vast majority by adequate governmental action.

— **Bertrand Russell**

Every decent man is ashamed of the government he lives under.

— **H.L. Mencken**

Disbelief in magic can force a poor soul into believing in government and business.

— **Tom Robbins**

The mystery of government is not how Washington works but how to make it stop.

— **P. J. O'Rourke**

For every action there is an equal and opposite government program.

— **Bob Wells**

I don't make jokes. I just watch the government and report the facts.

— **Will Rogers**

You will find that the State is the kind of organization which, though it does big things badly, does small things badly, too.

— **John Kenneth Galbraith**

There's no trick to being a humorist when you have the whole government working for you.

— **Will Rogers**

Sure there are dishonest men in local government. But there are dishonest men in national government too.

— **Richard M. Nixon**

It is dangerous to be right when the government is wrong.

— **Voltaire**

A government that robs Peter to pay Paul can always depend upon the support of Paul.

— **George Bernard Shaw**

The function of government is to provide you with service; the function of the media is to supply the Vaseline.

— **Ernest Hancock**

grammar
noun

1. A system of pitfalls thoughtfully prepared for the feet for the self-made man.

grandchildren
noun

1. God's reward for not killing your kids.

Children are God's punishment for having sex. And Grandchildren are God's reward for putting up with them.
— **Ronald Appel**

The reason grandparents and grandchildren get along so well is that they have a common enemy.
— **Sam Levenson**

gratitude
noun

1. Penitence for the ingrate.
2. The secret hope of further favor.

grave
noun

1. A place in which the dead await the coming of the medical student.

gravity
noun

1. The tendency of all bodies to approach one another with strength proportional to the quantity of matter they contain. The point of proof being that the skull of any politician or Hollywood star produces no gravity.

We can lick gravity, but sometimes the paperwork is overwhelming.
— **Wernher von Braun**

guillotine
noun

1. A machine which makes a Frenchman shrug his shoulders with good reason.

In his great work on Divergent Lines of Racial Evolution, the learned Professor Brayfugle argues from the prevalence of this gesture – the shrug – among Frenchmen, that they are descended from turtles and it is simply a survival of the habit of retracing the head inside the shell. It is with reluctance that I differ with so eminent an authority, but in my judgment the shrug is a poor foundation upon which to build so important a theory, for previously to the Revolution the gesture was unknown. I have not a doubt that it is directly referable to the terror inspired by the guillotine during the period of that instrument's activity.

— **Ambrose Bierce**

gun
noun

1. An agency employed by civilized nations for the settlement of disputes which might become troublesome if left unadjusted.

The end move in politics is always to pick up a gun.
— **Richard Buckminster Fuller**

You can go a long way with a smile. You can go a lot farther with a smile and a gun.
— **Al Capone**

The fascination of shooting as a sport depends almost wholly on whether you are at the right or wrong end of the gun.
— **P. G. Wodehouse**

gunshot
noun

1. A counterargument prepared for the demands of American Socialist.

guru
noun

1. A computer owner who can read the manual.

H. (As in "Hellish")

habeas corpus
noun

1. A writ by which a man may be taken out of jail when confined for the wrong crime.

habit
noun

1. A shackle for the free.

> The second half of a man's life is made up of nothing but the habits he has acquired during the first half.
> — **Fyodor Dostoevsky**

> My problem lies in reconciling my gross habits with my net income.
> — **Errol Flynn**

> Excess on occasion is exhilarating. It prevents moderation from acquiring the deadening effect of a habit.
> — **W. Somerset Maugham**

> Without the aid of prejudice and custom I should not be able to find my way across the room.
> — **William Hazlitt**

> A poet who reads his verse in public may have other nasty habits.
> — **Robert Heinlein**

Hades
noun

1. The place where the dead live (see Congress).

> Among the ancients the idea of Hades was not synonymous with our Hell, many of the most respectable men of antiquity residing there in a very comfortable kind of way. Indeed, the Elysian Fields them-

selves were a part of Hades, though they have since been removed to Paris.

— **Ambrose Bierce**

hag
noun

1. An elderly lady whom you do not happen to like (see Mother In-law).

hand
noun

1. A singular instrument worn at the end of the human arm and commonly thrust into somebody's pocket.

handkerchief
noun

1. A small square of silk or linen, used in various ignoble orifices about the face and especially serviceable at funerals to conceal the lack of tears.

happiness
noun

1. An agreeable sensation arising from contemplating the misery of another.
2. Bad memory.

All I ask is a chance to prove that money can't make me happy.

— **Unknown**

Money doesn't always bring happiness. People with ten million dollars are no happier than people with nine million dollars.

— **Hobart Brown**

One of the indictments of civilizations is that happiness and intelligence are so rarely found in the same person.

— **William Feather**

Happiness is having a large, loving, caring, close-knit family in another city.

— **George Burns**

Some cause happiness wherever they go; others whenever they go.

— **Oscar Wilde**

> There are lots of ways of being miserable, but there's only one way of being comfortable, and that is to stop running round after happiness. If you make up your mind not to be happy there's no reason why you shouldn't have a fairly good time.
> — **Edith Wharton**

harangue
noun

1. A speech by an opponent, who is known as a harangue-outang.

harbor
noun

1. A location for transients who imbibe in heavy drink and prostitution – indistinguishable from Congress.
2. A place where ships taking shelter from storms are exposed to the fury of Customs.

hatchet
noun

1. A young axe, suited for burial in the back of a friend.

hatred
noun

1. A sentiment useful in confirming another's superiority.

> Now hatred is by far the longest pleasure; Men love in haste, but they detest at leisure.
> — **Lord Byron**

hearse
noun

1. Death's baby carriage.

heart
noun

1. A natural magnet for daggers and bullets.

A man's heart is like a sponge, just soaked with emotion and sentiment of which he can squeeze a little bit out for every pretty woman.

— **Helen Rowland**

Figuratively, this useful organ is said to be the seat of emotions and sentiments – a very pretty fancy which, however, is nothing but a survival of a once universal belief. It is now known that the sentiments and emotions reside in the stomach, being evolved from food by chemical action of the gastric fluid. The exact process by which a beefsteak becomes a feeling – tender or not, according to the age of the animal from which it was cut; the successive stages of elaboration through which a caviar sandwich is transmuted to a quaint fancy and reappears as a pungent epigram; the marvelous functional methods of converting a hard-boiled egg into religious contrition, or a cream-puff into a sigh of sensibility – these things have been patiently ascertained by M. Pasteur, and by him expounded with convincing lucidity.

— **Ambrose Bierce**

Any woman who thinks the way to a man's heart is through his stomach is aiming about 10 inches too high.

— **Adrienne E. Gusoff**

The heart gets what the heart will settle for.

— **The Cleveland Show**

heathen
noun

1. A benighted creature who has the folly to worship something that he can see and feel.

heaven
noun

1. A place where the wicked cease from troubling you with talk of their personal affairs, and the good listen with attention while you expound your own.

In heaven all the interesting people are missing.

— **Friedrich Nietzsche**

It is a curious thing ... that every creed promises a paradise which will be absolutely uninhabitable for anyone of civilized taste.

— **Evelyn Waugh**

Hebrew
noun

1. A male Jew, as distinguished from the Shebrew, an altogether superior creation.

henpecked
noun

1. The natural order of (married) men.

hermit
noun

1. A person whose vices and follies are not sociable.

hers
pronoun

1. His.

> In divorce cases, the woman adopts the legal position that what is hers is hers, and what is his is hers.
> — **Andy Bernstein**

hibernate
noun

1. For wild animals, to pass the winter imitating an office worker.

historian
noun

1. A broad-gauge gossip.
2. An unsuccessful novelist.

> Any event, once it has occurred, can be made to appear inevitable by a competent historian.
> — **Lee Simonson**

Historians are like deaf people who go on answering questions that no one has asked them.
— Leo Tolstoy

history
noun

1. An account (mostly false) of events (mostly unimportant) which are brought about by rulers (mostly knaves) and soldiers (mostly fools).
2. The short period from Adam to atom.
3. The race between education and catastrophe.

> We learn from history that we do not learn from history.
> — Georg Wilhelm Friedrich Hegel

> Indeed, history is nothing more than a tableau of crimes and misfortunes.
> — Voltaire

> Events in the past may be roughly divided into those which probably never happened and those which do not matter.
> — W. R. Inge

> For four-fifths of our history, our planet was populated by pond scum.
> — J.W. Schopf

> History is a set of lies agreed upon
> — Napoleon Bonaparte

> In times like these, it helps to recall that there have always been times like these.
> — Paul Harvey

hitchhiker
noun

1. One who avoids hiking by hitching.

Hollywood
noun

1. A region populated by professional liars of an order that celebrates dysfunctional behavior.

It's hard to tell where Hollywood ends and the DTs begin.
— **W.C. Fields**

After two years in Washington, I often long for the realism and sincerity of Hollywood.
— **Fred Thompson (actor and Senator)**

You can take all the sincerity in Hollywood, place it in the navel of a firefly and still have room enough for three caraway seeds and a producer's heart.
— **Fred Allen**

Hollywood is a place where they'll pay you a thousand dollars for a kiss and fifty cents for your soul.
— **Marilyn Monroe**

Behind the phony tinsel of Hollywood lies the real tinsel.
— **Oscar Levant**

You can't find any true closeness in Hollywood, because everybody does the fake closeness so well.
— **Carrie Fisher**

In Hollywood a marriage is a success if it outlasts milk.
— **Rita Rudner**

Hollywood is a place where they place you under contract instead of under observation.
— **Walter Winchell**

Small towns in the United States are the repositories of American nostalgia. The big cities are laboratories of American pathology. For pathological nostalgia, we have Hollywood.
— **William Ferraiolo**

homeless
adjective

1. Having paid all taxes on household goods.

homicide
noun

1. Darwinism by unnatural selection.

There are four kinds of homicide: felonious, excusable, justifiable, and praiseworthy, but it makes no great difference to the person slain whether he fell by one kind or another – the classification is for advantage of the lawyers.

— **Ambrose Bierce**

honesty
noun

1. The first form of self-destructive behavior.

2. That which a woman may ask for, but rarely truly desires.

3. Information imparted without editing for personal advantage (a.k.a. failed strategy)

Honesty is one of the better policies

— **Ralph Seifert**

Honesty may be the best policy, but it's important to remember that apparently, by elimination, dishonesty is the second-best policy.

— **George Carlin**

Honesty is the best image.

— **Tom Wilson**

The intellectual honesty of a wealthy clergy is best demonstrated when hung from a gibbet.

— **Jon Digerness**

It is amazing the number of people who are pleased by the simple act of sincerely professing the truth. I mean, I would have thought there would have been at least one.

— **John Alejandro King**

An honest politician is one who, when he is bought, will stay bought.

— **Simon Cameron**

Honesty is a good thing, but it is not profitable to its possessor unless it is kept under control.

— **Don Marquis**

Honesty pays, but it doesn't seem to pay enough to suit some people.

— **F. M. Hubbard**

It is inaccurate to say that I hate everything. I am strongly in favor of common sense, common honesty, and common decency. This makes me forever ineligible for public office.
— **H.L. Mencken**

It is possible that the percentage of honest and competent whores is higher than that of plumbers and much higher than that of lawyers.
— **Robert Heinlein**

honorable
adjective

1. Afflicted with an impediment in one's reach, limited to a distance short of another person's property.

If a man speaks of his honor, make him pay cash.
— **Robert Heinlein**

In legislative bodies it is customary to mention all members as honorable; as "the honorable gentleman is a scurvy cur."
— **Ambrose Bierce**

hope
noun

1. Desire and expectation rolled into one.
2. Tomorrow's veneer over today's disappointment.

In our factory, we make lipstick. In our advertising, we sell hope.
— **Charles Revlon**

horse
noun

1. A creature beautiful at one end, disgusting at the other, and uncomfortable in the middle.

hospitality
noun

1. The virtue which induces us to feed and lodge certain persons who are not in need of food and lodging.

hostility
noun

1. An external representation of the earth's overpopulation.

> Hostility is classified as active and passive; as (respectively) the feeling of a woman for her female friends, and that which she entertains for all the rest of her sex.
> **— Ambrose Bierce**

house
noun

1. A hollow edifice erected for the habitation of man, rat, mouse, beetle, cockroach, fly, mosquito, flea, bacillus, and microbe.

human
noun

1. An animal with delusions of grandeur.
2. Technologically advanced breed of ape with delusions of civilization.
3. The only species disappointed in itself.
4. A species with a strong instinct for being unhappy at a highly developed level.

> Most human beings have an almost infinite capacity for taking things for granted.
> **— Aldous Huxley**

> Human nature is wanting what you can't have, and having what you don't want.
> **— Unknown**

> Human beings are seventy percent water, and with some the rest is collagen.
> **— Martin Mull**

> To err is human; to forgive, infrequent.
> **— Franklin P. Adams**

Human beings, who are almost unique in having the ability to learn from the experience of others, are also remarkable for their apparent disinclination to do so.

— **Douglas Adams**

The chief obstacle to the progress of the human race is the human race.

— **Don Marquis**

To err is human – and to blame it on a computer is even more so.

— **Robert Orben**

Humans are the only animals that have children on purpose with the exception of guppies, who like to eat theirs.

— **P.J. O'Rourke**

Humans are not the end result of predictable evolutionary progress, but rather a fortuitous cosmic afterthought, a tiny little twig on the enormously arborescent bush of life, which if replanted from seed, would almost surely not grow this twig again.

— **Stephen J. Gould**

humanity

noun

1. A virus with shoes.

2. The human race, collectively, exclusive of lawyers.

The urge to save humanity is almost always only a false-face for the urge to rule it.

— **H.L. Mencken**

Humanity has advanced, when it has advanced, not because it has been sober, responsible, and cautious, but because it has been playful, rebellious, and immature.

— **Tom Robbins**

humility

noun

1. The embarrassment felt when telling others how wonderful you are.

Life is a long lesson in humility.

— **James M. Barrie**

husband
noun

1. What remains of a lover after the nerve has been removed.
2. One who having dined, is charged with the cleaning of the plates.

A husband is like a fire, he goes out when unattended.
— **Evan Esar**

One good husband is worth two good wives; for the scarcer things are, the more they are valued.
— **Benjamin Franklin**

What's the difference between a boyfriend and a husband? About 30 pounds.
— **Cindy Gardner**

American women expect to find in their husbands a perfection that English women only hope to find in their butlers.
— **W. Somerset Maugham**

 (AS IN "IRREDEEMABLE")

iconoclast
noun

1. A cynic with social skills so poor that he brings sight to the blind.

idealism
noun

1. What precedes experience, not to be confused with what follows experience, namely cynicism.

idealist
noun

1. One who, on noticing that a rose smells better than a cabbage, concludes that it will also make better soup.
2. A person who helps other people to be prosperous.

> Cynics regarded everybody as equally corrupt. Idealists regarded everybody as equally corrupt, except themselves.
> — **Robert Anton Wilson**

idiot
noun

1. The stock analyst that just downgraded your largest holding.
2. A member of a large and powerful tribe whose influence in human affairs has always been dominant and controlling.

> The world is run by idiots because they're more efficient than hamsters.
> — **Unknown**

Programming today is a race between software engineers striving to build bigger and better idiot-proof programs, and the Universe trying to produce bigger and better idiots. So far, the Universe is winning.

— **Rich Cook**

Suppose you were an idiot and suppose you were a member of Congress. But I repeat myself.

— **Mark Twain**

The Idiot's activity is not confined to any special field of thought or action, but "pervades and regulates the whole." He has the last word in everything; his decision is unappealable. He sets the fashions and opinion of taste, dictates the limitations of speech and circumscribes conduct with a dead-line.

— **Ambrose Bierce**

idol
noun

1. A false god worshiped by heathens as opposed to the One True God, worshiped by false followers.

ignoramus
noun

1. A person unacquainted with certain kinds of knowledge familiar to yourself, and having certain other kinds that you know nothing about.

ignorant
adjective

1. Someone who doesn't know what you have just learned.

Against logic there is no armor like ignorance.

— **Laurence J. Peter**

Beware of the man who works hard to learn something, learns it, and finds himself no wiser than before. He is full of murderous resentment of people who are ignorant without having come by their ignorance the hard way.

— **Bokonon**

Men are born ignorant, not stupid; they are made stupid by education.
— **Bertrand Russell**

It is impossible to defeat an ignorant man in argument.
— **William G. McAdoo**

illuminati
noun

1. Idiots who have gained their status through education beyond their capacity.

illustrious
adjective

1. Suitably placed for the shafts of malice, envy, and detraction.

imagination
noun

1. A factory feed by minor facts, with a poet and a liar in joint ownership.

Anyone who lives within their means suffers from a lack of imagination.
— **Oscar Wilde**

Imagination is the one weapon in the war against reality.
— **Jules de Gaultier**

Skill without imagination is craftsmanship and gives us many useful objects such as wickerwork picnic baskets. Imagination without skill gives us modern art.
— **Tom Stoppard**

Imbecility
noun

1. The mental state of the critics of this book.

imitation
noun

1. The sincerest form of television and politics.

When people are free to do as they please, they usually imitate each other.
— Eric Hoffer

immigrant
noun

1. An unenlightened person who thinks one country is better than another.

immodest
adjective

1. Having a strong sense of one's own merit, coupled with a feeble conception of worth in others.

immoral
adjective

1. Inexpedient.

2. Involved in vices other than one's neighbors.

immortality
noun

1. The ultimate perpetuation of boredom.

2. Eternal ennui.

Millions long for immortality who don't know what to do with themselves on a rainy Sunday afternoon.
— Susan Ertz

The only thing wrong with immortality is that it tends to go on forever.
— Herb Caen

Immortality can always be assured by spectacular error.
— John Kenneth Galbraith

impartial
adjective

1. Unable to perceive any promise of personal advantage from espousing either side of a controversy or adopting either of two conflicting opinions.

impiety
noun

1. Your irreverence toward my deity.

impunity
noun

1. Wealth.

income
noun

1. An economic that you can't live without or within.
2. The natural and rational gauge and measure of respectability.

> Anyone who lives within their means suffers from a lack of imagination.
> — **Oscar Wilde**

> There is nothing more demoralizing than a small but adequate income.
> — **Edmund Wilson**

> All progress is based upon a universal innate desire on the part of every organism to live beyond its income.
> — **Samuel Butler**

incompatibility
noun

1. In matrimony, a similarity of tastes, particularly the taste for domination.

incumbent
noun

1. The candidate to vote against.

indifference
noun

1. The essence of both humanity and inhumanity.

indifferent
adjective

1. Imperfectly sensible to distinction among things.

ineptocracy
noun

1. A system of government where the least capable of leading are elected by the least capable of deciding.

inexorable
adjective

1. Not to be persuaded or moved by entreaty, prayer, logic, threats, begging, manipulation, psychological torture, or acts of physical violence … though bribery is still an option.

inexpedient
adjective

1. Not calculated to advance one's interests.

infancy
noun

1. The period of our lives immediately before the world begins lying to us and about us.

infidel
noun

1. One who does not subscribe to the local myths. In New York, one who does not believe in the Christian religion; in Baghdad, one who does.

inflation
noun

1. Cutting money in half without damaging the paper.
2. The only known economic phenomenon whereby the rich do not get richer.

influence
noun

1. In politics, a visionary "quo" given in exchange for a substantial "quid".

> Clothes make the man. Naked people have little or no influence on society.
> — **Mark Twain**

ingrate
noun

1. One who receives a benefit from another, or is otherwise an object of charity.

ink
noun

1. A villainous compound chiefly used to facilitate the infection of idiocy and promote intellectual crime.

> The properties of ink are peculiar and contradictory: it may be used to make reputations and unmake them; to blacken them and to make them white; but it is most generally and acceptably employed as a mortar to bind together the stones of an edifice of fame, and as a whitewash to conceal afterward the rascal quality of the material. There are men called journalists who have established ink baths which some persons pay money to get into, others to get out of. Not infrequently it occurs that a person who has paid to get in pays twice as much to get out.
> — **Ambrose Bierce**

insanity
noun

1. Doing the same thing over and over again and expecting different results.

> Many people hear voices when no-one is there. Some of them are called mad and are shut up on rooms where they stare at the walls all

day. Others are called writers and they do pretty much the same thing.

— **Meg Chittenden**

What garlic is to salad, insanity is to art.

— **Unknown**

The more things change, the more they remain ... insane.

— **Michael Fry & T. Lewis**

Insanity in individuals is something rare – but in groups, parties, nations and epochs, it is the rule. [Editor: He forgot *committees*]

— **Friedrich Nietzsche**

institutional investor
noun

1. A reformed investor in charge of an asylum.

insurance
noun

1. An ingenious modern game of chance in which the player is permitted to enjoy the comfortable conviction that he is beating the man who owns the casino.

insurrection
noun

1. An unsuccessful revolution.
2. A patriotic attempt to substitute anarchy for bad government.

intellectual
noun

1. A person who takes more words than necessary to tell more than he knows.
2. Someone who prefers theory over experience, so much so that they would sit on a hot stove twice.

An intellectual is a person who has discovered something more interesting than sex.

— **Aldous Huxley**

The avoidance of taxes is the only intellectual pursuit that carries any reward.

— **John Maynard Keynes**

Internet
noun

1. An electronic system for interconnecting computers around the world, and thus providing faster and more reliable ways for crashing them.
2. A vast suppository of information.

My favorite thing about the Internet is that you get to go into the private world of real creeps without having to smell them.

— **Penn Jillette**

We've heard that a million monkeys at a million keyboards could produce the complete works of Shakespeare; now, thanks to the Internet, we know that is not true.

— **Robert Wilensky**

The Internet is like having at your disposal the largest library in the world, but a library where someone comes in every night and rearranges the books at random.

— **Unknown**

intimacy
noun

1. A relation into which fools are providentially drawn for their mutual destruction.

introduction
noun

1. A social ceremony for the gratification of the host and the plaguing of his guests.

The introduction attains its most malevolent development in this century, being, indeed, closely related to our political system. Every American being the equal of every other American, it follows that everybody has the right to know everybody else, which implies the right to introduce without request or permission. The Declaration of

Independence should have read thus: "We hold these truths to be self-evident: that all men are created equal; that they are endowed by their Creator with certain inalienable rights; that among these are life, and the right to make that of another miserable by thrusting upon him an incalculable quantity of acquaintances; liberty, particularly the liberty to introduce persons to one another without first ascertaining if they are not already acquainted as enemies; and the pursuit of another's happiness with a running pack of strangers."

— **Ambrose Bierce**

invention
noun

1. The mother of necessity.

He who builds a better mousetrap these days runs into material shortages, patent-infringement suits, work stoppages, collusive bidding, discount discrimination and taxes.

— **H. E. Martz**

Getting caught is the mother of invention.

— **Robert Byrne**

invoice
noun

1. Documents that travels through the mail at twice the speed of payments.

irregardlessness
adverb

1. A state of having no regard for anything, including the standards of English.

J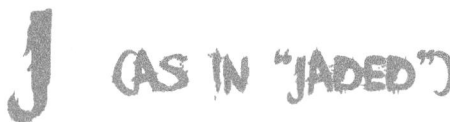

jealous
adjective

1. Unduly concerned about the preservation of that which can be lost only if not worth keeping.

> Moral indignation is jealousy with a halo.
> — H. G. Wells

jester
noun

1. Someone fool of himself.
2. An officer attached to a king's household, whose business it was to amuse the court by ludicrous actions and utterances, often indistinguishable from the monarch.

journalism
noun

1. Informing the public that a person is dead when the public never knew that the person was ever alive.

> Rock journalism is people who can't write interviewing people who can't talk for people who can't read.
> — Frank Zappa

judge
noun

1. A law student who grades his own examination papers.
2. A member of the bar who once knew a governor.

Judges without convictions are the most generous in handing them out.

— **Unknown**

Junk
noun

1. That thing (or things) you've kept for years and throw away three weeks before you need it.

jury
noun

1. Twelve people chosen to decide who has the better lawyer.

We have a criminal jury system which is superior to any in the world; and its efficiency is only marred by the difficulty of finding twelve men every day who don't know anything and can't read.

— **Mark twain**

When you go into court you are putting your fate into the hands of twelve people who weren't smart enough to get out of jury duty.

— **Norm Crosby**

The penalty for laughing in a courtroom is six months in jail; if it were not for this penalty, the jury would never hear the evidence.

— **H.L. Mencken**

justice
noun

1. A lady subjected to so many miscarriages that her virtue is in doubt.
2. A commodity, usually adulterated, that the State sells to the citizen as a reward for his allegiance, taxes, and personal service.

If life was fair, Elvis would be alive and all the impersonators would be dead.

— **Johnny Carson**

A man's respect for law and order exists in precise relationship to the size of his paycheck.

— **Adam Clayton Powell Jr.**

Military justice is to justice what military music is to music.
— **Groucho Marx**

If my fellow citizens want to go to hell, I will help them. That is my job.
— **Justice Oliver Wendell Holmes**

 (AS IN "KNOWING")

kill
transitive verb

1. To create a vacancy without nominating a successor.

> To kill one person is murder. To kill thousands is foreign policy.
> — **Moh-Tze**

> They say you can kill a man, but you can't kill an idea. I say: Any man I want to?
> — **John Alejandro King**

> Never ask for more money than it would take to have you killed by a professional.
> — **Unknown**

kilt
noun

1. A costume sometimes worn by Scotsmen in America and Americans in Scotland.

kindness
noun

1. A preface to extortion.

> One can always be kind to people about whom one cares nothing.
> — **Oscar Wilde**

king
noun

1. A male person commonly known in America as a "crowned head", although in England, he never wears a crown and in France, has usually no head.

kiss
noun

1. An upper persuasion, for a lower invasion.

> People who throw kisses are hopelessly lazy.
> — **Bob Hope**

> Hollywood is a place where they'll pay you a thousand dollars for a kiss and fifty cents for your soul.
> — **Marilyn Monroe**

kleptomaniac
noun

1. A rich thief.
2. A person who helps himself because he can't help himself.
3. A thief driven by motives less offensive, but less pure than greed.

L (AS IN "LEERY")

labor
noun

1. One of the processes by which A acquires property for B.

> There is no expedient to which a man will not go to avoid the labor of thinking.
> — **Thomas A. Edison**

landslide
noun

1. Term in political science, used by winning candidates who receive at least 50.00001% of the vote.

language
noun

1. The source of misunderstandings.
2. The music with which we charm the serpents guarding another's treasure.

> The Romans would never have found time to conquer the world if they had been obliged first to learn Latin.
> — **Heinrich Heine**

> If the English language made any sense, a catastrophe would be an apostrophe with fur.
> — **Doug Larson**

> England and America are two countries separated by the same language.
> — **George Bernard Shaw**

> God burdened man with multiple languages to slow our progress, for only God knows how really ^%((&#* dangerous we are.
> — **Guy Smith**

Man invented language to satisfy his deep need to complain.
— **Lily Tomlin**

The great thing about human language is that it prevents us from sticking to the matter at hand.
— **Lewis Thomas**

law
noun

1. The tool of an enlightened society for regulating theft.

A man's respect for law and order exists in precise relationship to the size of his paycheck.
— **Adam Clayton Powell Jr.**

The United States is a nation of laws: badly written and randomly enforced.
— **Frank Zappa**

Laws are like sausages. It's better not to see them being made.
— **Otto von Bismarck**

The problem with any unwritten law is that you don't know where to go to erase it.
— **Glaser and Way**

To succeed in the trades, capacity must be shown; in the law, concealment of it will do.
— **Mark Twain**

lawful
adjective

1. Compatible with the will of a judge having jurisdiction.

lawyer
noun

1. One skilled in circumvention of the law.

2. Someone who helps you get what is coming to him.

3. A person who extracts the truth from a situation before concealing it.

4. Someone who defends your interest and takes the principal.

5. A liar with a permit to practice.

> We joke but deep-down, lawyers are not bad people. I'd have to say right around six-feet deep is when they are not so bad.
> — **Mark Wonsil**

> Lawyers spend a great deal of their time shoveling smoke.
> — **Oliver Wendell Holmes Jr.**

> The only funny thing about lawyer jokes is that lawyers don't think they're funny, and everyone else doesn't know that they're jokes.
> — **Many Lawyers**

> A lawyer starts life giving $500 worth of law for $5 and ends giving $5 worth for $500.
> — **Benjamin H. Brewster**

> It has been said that we joke about those that we truly love. This is bunk, for there is no book thicker than the book of lawyer jokes.
> — **Guy Smith**

> It is possible that the percentage of honest and competent whores is higher than that of plumbers and much higher than that of lawyers.
> — **Robert Heinlein**

> One would have thought litigation superior to dueling for the purpose of settling disputes – provided that one had not met a lawyer.
> — **William Ferraiolo**

> Lawyers are always more ready to get a man into troubles than out of them.
> — **Oliver Goldsmith**

> Possession is nine points of the law. Lawyer fees and the other ninety one.
> — **Unknown**

> No poet ever interpreted nature as freely as a lawyer interprets the truth.
> — **Jean Giraudoux**

> If it weren't for the lawyers we wouldn't need them.
> — **William Jennings Bryan**

laziness
noun

1. The natural state of man before marriage.

> Laziness is nothing more than the habit of resting before you get tired.
> — **Jules Renard**

> Efficiency is intelligent laziness.
> — **David Dunham**

> For many (people) doing nothing would be an improvement.
> — **William Ferraiolo**

lead
noun

1. A heavy blue-gray metal much used in giving stability to lovers who love other men's wives. Lead is also of great service as a counterpoint to an argument.

learning
noun

1. The kind of ignorance displayed by the studious.

> We learn from history that we do not learn from history.
> — **Georg Wilhelm Friedrich Hegel**

> Human beings, who are almost unique in having the ability to learn from the experience of others, are also remarkable for their apparent disinclination to do so.
> — **Douglas Adams**

lecturer
noun

1. A person with his hand in your pocket, his tongue in your ear, and his faith in your patience.

liar

noun

1. A lawyer who has secured his retainer.

> It is always the best policy to speak the truth – unless, of course, you are an exceptionally good liar.
> — **Jerome K. Jerome**

> The income tax has made liars out of more Americans than golf.
> — **Will Rogers**

> We often hope that our elected officials are lying to us, because the alternative is that they really are the rank imbeciles that they appear to be.
> — **William Ferraiolo**

liberal

noun

1. Someone who does not care what you do as long as it is compulsory.
2. A person who feels a great debt to his fellow man, which he proposes to pay-off with your money.
3. A person whose interests aren't at stake at the moment.
4. A person too broadminded to take his own side in a quarrel.
5. A school of thought loved by people, but hated by Republicans.
6. A statesman that strives to replace current evils with fresh, new evils.

> It only takes 20 years for a liberal to become a conservative without changing a single idea.
> — **Robert Anton Wilson**

> Liberals are very broadminded: they are always willing to give careful consideration to both sides of the same side.
> — **Unknown**

liberty

noun

1. One of imagination's most precious possessions.

Liberty means responsibility. That is why most men dread it.
— George Barnard Shaw

No man's life, liberty or property are safe while the legislature is in session.
— Judge Gideon J. Tucker

lie
noun

1. Truth told from a convenient perspective.

Actions lie louder than words.
— Carolyn Wells

Never believe anything until it has been officially denied.
— Claud Cockburn

A lie can travel halfway around the world while the truth is putting on its shoes.
— Mark Twain

It is hard to believe that a man is telling the truth when you know that you would lie if you were in his place.
— H.L. Mencken

In order to preserve your self-respect, it is sometimes necessary to lie and cheat.
— Robert Byrne

There are three kinds of lies: lies, damned lies, and statistics.
— Benjamin Disraeli

Everybody lies, but it doesn't matter because nobody listens.
— Nick Diamos

Lies are like children: they're hard work, but it's worth it because the future depends on them.
— Pam Davis

life
noun

1. A strange, inconvenient, and unpopular restaurant where waiters bring you things you did not order and do not like.
2. An always fatal, sexually transmitted disease.

3. A foreign language that everyone mispronounces.

4. A zoo in a jungle.

> Life is a sports car – fast, sleek, majestic zipping through the continuum of time with the entire universe viewable through a gleaming and utterly transparent windshield. We are the bugs on that windshield.
> — **Guy Smith**

> Life isn't fair. It's just fairer than death, that's all.
> — **William Goldman**

> The only thing that makes life possible is permanent, intolerable uncertainty.
> — **Ursula K. LeGuin**

> Life – the way it really is – is a battle not between Bad and Good but between Bad and Worse.
> — **Joseph Brodsky**

> Life is a wonderful thing to talk about, or to read about in history books – but it is terrible when one has to live it.
> — **Jean Anouilh**

> It's not true that life is one damn thing after another; it is one damn thing over and over.
> — **Edna St. Vincent Millay**

> The supreme irony of life is that hardly anyone gets out of it alive.
> — **Robert Heinlein**

> Things are going to get a lot worse before they get worse.
> — **Lily Tomlin**

> We are born wet, naked, and hungry . . . then things get worse.
> — **Charles Gilbert**

> I got through life on partial credit.
> — **Dave Preston**

> Life is nothing but a competition to be the criminal rather than the victim.
> — **Bertrand Russell**

> In spite of the cost of living, it's still popular.
> — **Laurence J. Peter**

For most men life is a search for the proper manila envelope in which to get themselves filed.
— **Clifton Fadiman**

Not a shred of evidence exists in favor of the idea that life is serious.
— **Brendan Gill**

Life is pleasant. Death is peaceful. It's the transition that's troublesome.
— **Isaac Asimov**

Life is just a bowl of pits.
— **Rodney Dangerfield**

Is there life after birth?
— **Guy Smith**

Life is a cement trampoline.
— **Howard Nordberg**

Life is a moderately good play with a badly written third act.
— **Truman Capote**

There must be more to life than having everything.
— **Maurice Sendak**

Sooner or later we're going to have to ask ourselves whether it is possible to make life more meaningful without charging it to Visa.
— **Daron Hicklin**

lighthouse
noun

1. A tall building on the seashore in which the government maintains a lamp and the son-in-law of a politician.

literature
noun

1. A perpetual processes of proving one's talent to people who lack such.

A classic is something that everybody wants to have read and nobody has read.
— **Mark Twain**

In literature as in love, we are astonished at what is chosen by others.
— **Andre Maurois**

litigant
noun

1. A person about to give up his skin for the hope of retaining his bones.
2. A person who fails to realize that the only party who makes money through litigation is the lawyer.

> The plaintiff and the defendant in an action of law are like two men ducking their heads in a bucket, and daring each other to remain longest under water.
> **— Samuel Johnson**

litigation
noun

1. A machine which you go into as a pig and come out of as a sausage.

> One would have thought litigation superior to dueling for the purpose of settling disputes – provided that one had not met a lawyer.
> **— William Ferraiolo**

lock
noun

1. The distinguishing device of civilization and the acknowledgement of its failure.

logic
noun

1. The art of being wrong with confidence (see Statistics).
2. The art of thinking and reasoning in strict accordance with the limitations and incapacities of the human misunderstanding.

> Against logic there is no armor like ignorance.
> **— Laurence J. Peter**
>
> If the world were a logical place, men would ride horses sidesaddle.
> **— Unknown**

We live in a Newtonian world of Einsteinian physics ruled by Frankenstein logic.
— **David Russell**

longevity
noun

1. Uncommon extension of the fear of death.

lord
noun

1. In American society, an English tourist above the status of a fishmonger.
2. Sometimes used, also, as a title of the Supreme Being; but this is thought to be flattery rather than true reverence.

lottery
noun

1. A system of voluntary taxation that extracts government revenue from the working poor whom otherwise are exempt, and the middle class whom are immune from understanding how thoroughly taxed they already are.

I've done the calculation and your chances of winning the lottery are identical whether you play or not.
— **Fran Lebowitz**

How come you never see a headline like "Psychic Wins Lottery"?
— **Jay Leno**

There are few things in this world more reassuring that an unhappy lottery winner.
— **Tony Parsons**

love
noun

1. The triumph of imagination over intelligence.
2. The painful realization that something other than oneself is real.
3. An interval between meeting a beautiful girl and discovering that she looks like a haddock.
4. A temporary insanity curable by marriage.

5. The irresistible desire to be irresistibly desired.

A man can be happy with any woman as long as he does not love her.

— **Oscar Wilde**

I so enjoy seeing young lovers smooching in public. Not only does it fill the heart with warm and sentimental feelings, but I'm comforted in the knowledge that the ship of their affections will soon sink on the rock shores of reality, or sucked forever downward in the maelstrom of marriage.

— **Guy Smith**

War is like love; it always finds a way.

— **Unknown**

There are three sure signs of love. The fire in the heart, the fire in the groin, and cross-fire when the other lover is discovered.

— **Guy Smith**

Love is what happens to a man and woman who don't know each other.

— **W. Somerset Maugham**

Love is like an hourglass, with the heart filling up as the brain empties.

— **Jules Renard**

Man and wife make one fool.

— **Ben Jonson**

Love is a severe mental disorder.

— **Plato**

Love is a snowmobile racing across the tundra and then suddenly it flips over, pinning you underneath. At night, the ice weasels come.

— **Matt Groening**

It is better to have loved and lost than never to have lost at all.

— **Samuel Butler**

To be happy with a man, you must understand him a lot and love him a little. To be happy with a woman, you must love her a lot and not try to understand her at all.

— **Helen Rowland**

Love is an exploding cigar we willingly smoke.

— **Lynda Barry**

[Love] This disease, like many other ailments, is prevalent only among civilized races living under artificial conditions; barbarous nations breathing pure air and eating simple food enjoy immunity from its ravages. It is sometimes fatal, but more frequently to the physician than to the patient.
— **Ambrose Bierce**

Love is a matter of chemistry, but sex is a matter of physics.
— **Unknown**

Love is blind, marriage is an eye opener, divorce is corrective ocular surgery.
— **Guy Smith**

There is a difference between loving a woman and falling in love with a woman. It is like the difference between admiring the mechanical design of a bear trap and stepping on it.
— **Guy Smith**

The man of knowledge must be able not only to love his enemies but also to hate his friends.
— **Friedrich Nietzsche**

First love is a kind of vaccination which saves a man from catching the complaint a second time.
— **Honore de Balzac**

luminary
noun

1. One who throws light upon a subject; as an editor, by not writing about it.

lunarian
noun

1. An inhabitant of the moon, as distinguished from lunatic, one whom the moon inhabits.

lying
adjective

1. Addicted to rhetoric.

Lying increases the creative faculties, expands the ego, and lessens the frictions of social contacts.

— **Clare Booth Luce**

---

lyre
noun

1. An ancient instrument of torture. The word is now used in a figurative sense to denote the poetic flaccidity.

M (AS IN "MOCKING")

mace
noun

1. A staff of office signifying authority, in its form of a heavy club that indicates its original purpose for dissuading dissent.

mad
adjective

1. Affected with a high degree of intellectual independence.

2. At odds with the majority.

3. Not conforming to standards of thought, speech, and action derived by conformant people from study of themselves.

4. A negative emotional state typically induced by the success of our enemies.

> Every man is wise when attacked by a mad dog; fewer when pursued by a mad woman.
> — **Robertson Davies**

> Sanity is a madness put to good use.
> — **George Santayana**

magic
noun

1. An art of converting superstition into income.

> Disbelief in magic can force a poor soul into believing in government and business.
> — **Tom Robbins**

> Formerly, when religion was strong and science weak, men mistook magic for medicine; now, when science is strong and religion weak, men mistake medicine for magic.
> — **Thomas Szasz**

magnificent
adjective

1. Having a grandeur or splendor superior to that to which the spectator is accustomed, as the glory of a maggot to a politician.

magpie
noun

1. A bird whose thieving ways suggests that it might be taught to talk.

maid
noun

1. A youngerly person of the fair sex employed to be variously disagreeable and ingeniously unclean.

maiden
noun

1. A young person of the unfair sex addicted to clueless conduct and views that madden to crime.

> The genus maiden has a wide geographical distribution, being found wherever sought and deplored wherever found. The maiden is not altogether unpleasing to the eye, nor (without her piano and her views) insupportable to the ear, though in respect to comeliness distinctly inferior to the rainbow, and, with regard to the part of her that is audible, bleating out of the field by the canary – which, also, is more portable.
>
> **— Ambrose Bierce**

male
noun

1. A member of the unconsidered, or negligible sex. The male of the human race is commonly known (to the female) as Mere Man. The genus, according to female biologists, has two varieties: good providers and exes.

The male is a domestic animal which, if treated with firmness, can be trained to do most things.

— **Jilly Cooper**

In politics, if you want anything said, ask a man – if you want anything done, ask a woman.

— **Margaret Thatcher**

mammalia
noun

1. A family of vertebrate animals whose females, in a state of nature, suckle their young, but when civilized and enlightened put them out to nurse, or use the bottle.

man
noun

1. An animal so lost in contemplation of what he thinks he is as to overlook what he ought to be.
2. An animal so clever it behaves like an imbecile.
3. A rational animal that loses its temper when called upon to act in accordance with the dictates of reason.

A woman can fake an orgasm, but it takes a man to fake an entire relationship.

— **Unknown**

History teaches us that men and nations behave wisely once they have exhausted all other alternatives.

— **Abba Eban**

Man is the only animal that can remain on friendly terms with the victims he intends to eat until he eats them.

— **Samuel Butler**

It is even harder for the average ape to believe that he has descended from man.

— **H.L. Mencken**

The more I study religions the more I am convinced that man never worshipped anything but himself.

— **Sir Richard Francis Burton**

If you pick up a starving dog and make him prosperous, he will not bite you. This is the principle difference between a dog and a man.
— **Mark twain**

I think that God in creating Man somewhat overestimated his ability.
— **Oscar Wilde**

Man is the only animal that blushes. Or needs to.
— **Mark Twain**

Man is living proof that God has a sense humor – he gave him two heads and only enough blood to think with one at a time.
— **Robin Williams**

[Man's] chief occupation is extermination of other animals and his own species, which, however, multiplies with such insistent rapidity as to infest the whole habitable earth and Canada.
— **Ambrose Bierce**

management
noun

1. The art of keeping employees who hate you away from those still making up their minds.

Lots of folks confuse bad management with destiny.
— **Kim Hubbard**

So much of what we call management consists in making it difficult for people to work.
— **Peter Drucker**

If at first you don't succeed, try management.
— **Unknown**

manna
noun

1. A food miraculously given to the Israelites in the wilderness. When it was no longer supplied to them they settled down and tilled the soil, fertilizing it, as a rule, with the bodies of the original occupants.

market correction
noun

1. The depression of stock prices precipitated by your purchasing stocks the day before.

marketing
verb

1. Techniques for intimidating or making people feel inadequate, so that they buy your product in order to compensate, often applied by women during courtship.

> Give a man a fish and he will eat for a day. Teach a man to fish and he will eat for a lifetime. Teach a man to create an artificial shortage of fish and he will eat steak.
> — **Jay Leno**

> Marketing science now seems to be advancing at a pace cancer research can only envy.
> — **Unknown**

> Market research can establish beyond the shadow of a doubt that the egg is a sad and sorry product and that it obviously will not continue to sell. Because after all, eggs won't stand up by themselves, they roll too easily, are too easily broken, require special packaging, look alike, are difficult to open, won't stack on the shelf.
> — **Robert Pliskin**

> "What if we had a war and nobody came?" Then marketing did a lousy job of promoting the event.
> — **Unknown**

marriage
noun

1. A fast funds transfer system.
2. Uncivil union.
3. The holy state of mutual disillusionment.
4. The state or condition of a community consisting of a master, a mistress and two slaves, making in all, two.
5. The only adventure open to cowards.

6. Nature's method of keeping us from fighting with strangers.

7. The mourning after the knot before.

> Financially speaking, being married with children is exactly like diving into a pond filled with leeches, except you can flick leech off.
> — **Scott Harrell and Guy Smith Jr.**

> Bachelors know more about women than married men; if they didn't they'd be married too.
> — **H.L. Mencken**

> Two can live as cheaply as one, for half as long.
> — **Unknown**

> I think men who have a pierced ear are better prepared for marriage. They've experienced pain and bought jewelry.
> — **Rita Rudner**

> A marriage without children is like a wound without salt.
> — **Bill Danzey**

> I know nothing about sex because I was always married.
> — **Zsa Zsa Gabor**

> I love being married. It's so great to find that one special person you want to annoy for the rest of your life.
> — **Rita Rudner**

> In Hollywood a marriage is a success if it outlasts milk.
> — **Rita Rudner**

> Some people claim that marriage interferes with romance. There's no doubt about it. Anytime you have a romance, your wife is bound to interfere.
> — **Groucho Marx**

> All marriages are happy. It's the living together afterward that causes all the trouble.
> — **Raymond Hull**

> After marriage, husband and wife become two sides of a coin; they just can't face each other, but still they stay together.
> — **Sasha Guitry**

> Love is blind, marriage is an eye opener, divorce is corrective ocular surgery.
> — **Guy Smith**

martyr
noun

1. One who follows the path of least reluctance to death.

martyrdom
noun

1. The only path to fame without ability.

maturity
noun

1. A quality which the young attempt to show and the old attempt to hide.
2. A short break in adolescence.
3. A point in time when we quit saying "I can" and start saying "I shouldn't", as in "I can drink a fifth of tequila!"

> I think age is a very high price to pay for maturity.
> — **Tom Stoppard**

> We are born charming, fresh and spontaneous and must be civilized before we are fit to participate in society.
> — **Judith Martin**

> We seldom become the people we want to be, but we always become the people that we try to be.
> — **Guy Smith**

mausoleum
noun

1. The final and funniest folly of the rich.

mayonnaise
noun

1. One of the sauces which serve the French in place of a state religion.

me
pronoun

1. The objectionable case of "I". The personal pronoun in English has three cases: the dominative, the objectionable, and the oppressive. Each is all three.

meda
noun

1. A small metal disk given as a reward for virtues, attainments, or services, occasionally authentic.

medicine
noun

1. A bullet fired in Florida to kill a dog in Alaska.

2. The art of amusing a patient while nature cures the disease.

> For all the advances in medicine, there is still no cure for the common birthday.
>
> — John Glenn

> Formerly, when religion was strong and science weak, men mistook magic for medicine; now, when science is strong and religion weak, men mistake medicine for magic.
>
> — Thomas Szasz

meekness
noun

1. Uncommon patience in planning a revenge that is worthwhile.

> The meek shall inherit the earth, in individual plots measuring six by three feet.
>
> — Paul Scott

meetings
noun

1. Addictive and self-indulgent activities that large organizations habitually engage in only because they cannot actually masturbate.

> Creativity dies a quick death in rooms with conference tables.
> — **Unknown**

> Meetings are indispensable when you don't want to do anything.
> — **John Kenneth Galbraith**

> Creativity dies a quick death in rooms with conference tables.
> — **Unknown**

memo
noun

1. Communication somewhere between an official document and a perfectly good blank sheet of paper.

> Bureaucrats write memoranda both because they appear to be busy when they are writing and because the memos, once written, immediately become proof that they were busy.
> — **Charles Peters**

menstruation
noun

1. A monthly physical condition that causes women to act like men always do.

mercy
noun

1. An attribute beloved of suspicious characters including judges, governors, and deities.

mesmerism
noun

1. Hypnotism before it wore good clothes, kept a carriage, and asked Incredulity to dine.

meteorologist
noun

1. A special (but not particular) kind of liar.

> Meteorologist exist to make astrologers look respectable by comparison.
> — Unknown

metropolis
noun

1. A rat's cage for Homo sapiens, often producing similar results.

millennium
noun

1. The period of time between one British summer and the next.

2. A period of 1,000 years between the resurrection of mass hysteria.

3. The launching pad for a 1,000 superstitions.

mine
adjective

1. Belonging to me if I can hold or seize it.

noun

2. A device for holding property (mainly land) by depriving others of their property (mainly legs).

minister
noun

1. In diplomacy, an officer sent into a foreign country as the visible embodiment of his sovereign's hostility. His principal qualification is a degree of feigned inveracity next below that of an ambassador.

2. In religion, an agent of a higher power with a lower responsibility.

miracle
noun

1. An act or event out of the order of nature and unaccountable, as beating a hand of four kings and an ace with four aces and a king.

miscreant
noun

1. A person of the highest degree of unworth, as in thief, drug addict, or office holder.

misdemeanor
noun

1. An infraction of the law having less dignity than a felony and constituting no claim to admittance into the best of criminal society, namely Congress.

miser
noun

1. A person who lives poor so that he can die rich.

> To be a book-collector is to combine the worst characteristics of a dope fiend with those of a miser.
> — **Robertson Davies**

> Every man serves a useful purpose: A miser, for example, makes a wonderful ancestor.
> — **Laurence J. Peter**

misfortune
noun

1. The kind of fortune that never misses.

> We all have strength enough to endure the misfortunes of others.
> — **Francois de La Rochefoucauld**

> Calamities are of two kinds: misfortunes to ourselves, and good fortune to others.
> — **Ambrose Bierce**

misogynist
noun

1. A man who hates every bone in a woman's body except his.
2. A man who hates women as much as women hate one another.

miss
noun

1. The title with which we brand unmarried women to indicate that they are in the cattle market of romance.

> Miss, Missis (Mrs.) and Mister (Mr.) are the three most distinctly disagreeable words in the language, in sound and sense. Two are corruptions of Mistress, the other of Master. In the general abolition of social titles in this our country they miraculously escaped to plague us. If we must have them let us be consistent and give one to the unmarried man. I venture to suggest Mush, abbreviated to Mh.
> — **Ambrose Bierce**

momentum investing
noun

1. The fine art of buying high and selling low.

monarch
noun

1. A person engaged in reigning.

> Formerly the monarch ruled, as the derivation of the word attests, and as many subjects have had occasion to learn. In Europe and other hostile regions, the monarch has still a considerable influence in public affairs and in the disposition of the human head, but in other political administrations is mostly entrusted to his ministers, he being somewhat preoccupied with reflections relating to the status of his own head.
> — **Ambrose Bierce (updated by Guy Smith)**

> An absolute monarchy is one in which the sovereign does as he pleases so long as he pleases the assassins. Not many absolute monarchies are left, most of them having been replaced by limited monarchies, where the sovereign's power for evil (and for good) is greatly curtailed, and by republics, which are governed by chance.
> — **Ambrose Bierce**

Monday
noun

1. A prototype for Hell.
2. The day after the ball game.

money
noun

1. A blessing having no advantage except when we part with it.
2. Evidence of culture and the passport to elite society.
3. Something you have to make in case you don't die.

> From birth to 18 a girl needs good parents. From 18 to 35, she needs good looks. From 35 to 55, good personality. From 55 on, she needs good cash.
> — **Sophie Tucker**

> If money is the root of all evil, why do churches keep begging for more?
> — **Unknown**

> Financially speaking, being married with children is exactly like diving into a pond filled with leeches, except you can flick leech off.
> — **Scott Harrell and Guy Smith Jr.**

> My wife says I spend money like a drunken sailor. Wonder what she'd say if I spent it like a sober congressman?"
> — **R. W. Plagge**

> Never ask for more money than it would take to have you killed by a professional.
> — **Unknown**

> The fundamental evil of the world arose from the fact that the good Lord has not created money enough.
> — **Heinrich Heine**

> Two can live as cheaply as one ... for half as long.
> — **Unknown**

> All I ask is a chance to prove that money can't make me happy.
> — **Unknown**

About the time we think we can make ends meet, somebody moves the ends.

— **Herbert Hoover**

Money is exactly like sex; You thought of nothing else if you didn't have it and thought of other things if you did.

— **James Baldwin**

I spent a lot of money on booze, birds, and fast cars. The rest I just squandered.

— **George Best**

Money doesn't always bring happiness. People with ten million dollars are no happier than people with nine million dollars.

— **Hobart Brown**

The tooth fairy teaches children that they can sell body parts for money.

— **David Richerby**

Money can't buy friends, but it can get you a better class of enemy.

— **Spike Milligan**

What this country needs is a good five-cent nickel.

— **Franklin P. Adams**

If you want to know what God thinks of money, just look at the people he gave it to.

— **Dorothy Parker**

Lack of money is the root of all evil.

— **George Bernard Shaw**

A billion here, a billion there, pretty soon it adds up to real money.

— **Senator Everett Dirksen**

Money is the sincerest form of flattery.

— **Robert Heinlein**

monkey
noun

1. An arboreal animal which makes itself at home in genealogical trees.

monosyllabic
adjective

1. Composed of words of one syllable, for literary babes and drug-addled individuals who never tire of torture (see Television Scriptwriter).

monument
noun

1. A structure dedicated to the memory of those who have left no memory.

moral
adjective

1. Conforming to a local (and transient) standard of "right", having the quality of expediency.

> The people who are regarded as moral luminaries are those who forego ordinary pleasures themselves and find compensation in interfering with the pleasures of others.
> **— Bertrand Russell**

> Moral indignation is jealousy with a halo.
> **— H. G. Wells**

> There is no moral precept that does not have something inconvenient about it.
> **— Denis Diderot**

morality
noun

1. The herd-instinct in the individual.

> We do not look in great cities for our best morality.
> **— Jane Austen**

> A man must be certain of his morality for the simple reason that he has to suffer for it.
> **— G. K. Chesterton**

> Never let your sense of morals get in the way of doing what's right.
> **— Isaac Asimov**

more
adjective

1. The comparative degree of too much.

morning
noun

1. A period of the day when the universe repeatedly whispers in your ear "screw you".

> I feel sorry for people who don't drink. When they wake up in the morning, that's as good as they're going to feel all day.
> **— Frank Sinatra**

> Eat a live toad the first thing in the morning and nothing worse will happen to you the rest of the day.
> **— Unknown**

Moses
noun

1. Biblical real estate agent.

mouse
noun

1. An animal which strews its path with fainting women and panicked pachyderms.

mouth
noun

1. In man, the gateway to the soul; in woman, the outlet of the Hades.

mugging
verb

1. The processes of forcing the surrender of the brain by shuttling coffee to the mouth via a mug.

mugwump
noun

1. A term of contempt used in politics to describe one afflicted with self-respect and addicted to the vice of independence.

multitude
noun

1. A mob; the raw materials of democracy, which is the poor cousin of a republic.
2. The object of the politician's adoration.

mummy
noun

1. An ancient Egyptian, now engaged by museums in gratifying the vulgar curiosity that serves to distinguish man from the lower animals.

musician
noun

1. A homeless man.

mustang
noun

1. A wild horse of the western plains. In English society, the American wife of an English nobleman.

myth
noun

1. A religion in which no one any longer believes.

mythology
noun

1. The body of a primitive people's beliefs concerning its origin, early history, heroes, deities and so forth, as distinguished from the true accounts which advanced civilizations invent later.

N (AS IN "NONBELIEVING")

nation
noun

1. A society united by delusions about its ancestry and by common hatred of its neighbors.

> History teaches us that men and nations behave wisely once they have exhausted all other alternatives.
> — **Abba Eban**
>
> The direct use of force is such a poor solution to any problem, it is generally employed only by small children and large nations.
> — **David Friedman**
>
> Every nation ridicules other nations, and all are right.
> — **Arthur Schopenhauer**

neighbor
noun

1. One whom we are commanded to love as ourselves, and who does everything possible to make us disobedient.

> The Bible tells us to love our neighbors, and also to love our enemies; probably because they are generally the same people.
> — **G. K. Chesterton**
>
> Love thy neighbor as yourself, but choose your neighborhood.
> — **Louise Beal**

nepotism
noun

1. The administrative process of appointing your grandmother to office for the good of the party.

neurosis
noun

1. A secret that you don't know you are keeping.

---

news
noun

1. The day to day reporting of nothing new.

> Of what you see in books, believe 75%. Of newspapers, believe 25%. And of TV news, believe 10% – make that 5% if the anchorman wears a blazer.
> — **Unknown**

> Television news is like a lightning flash. It makes a loud noise, lights up everything around it, leaves everything else in darkness and then is suddenly gone.
> — **Hodding Carter**

> For most folks, no news is good news; for the press, good news is not news.
> — **Gloria Borger**

> People everywhere confuse what they read in newspapers with news.
> — **A. J. Liebling**

> CNN is one of the participants in the war. I have a fantasy where Ted Turner is elected president but refuses because he doesn't want to give up power.
> — **Arthur C. Clarke**

> Trying to determine what is going on in the world by reading newspapers is like trying to tell the time by watching the second hand of a clock.
> — **Ben Hecht**

> The one function TV news performs very well is that when there is no news we give it to you with the same emphasis as if there were.
> — **David Brinkley**

> May you have the good fortune to die on a slow news day.
> — **Guy Smith**

nirvana
noun

1. In the Buddhist religion, a state of pleasurable annihilation awarded to the wise, obtained through unwise pursuits.

noise
noun

1. Undomesticated music.

2. A stench in the ear.

3. The chief product and authenticating sign of civilization.

nominate
verb

1. To designate for the heaviest political assault.

2. To place a suitable person as the target of public abuse.

nominee
noun

1. A modest person shrinking from the distinction of private life and diligently seeking the dishonorable obscurity of public office.

nonsense
noun

1. Any objection raised against this book.

> It is a far, far better thing to have a firm anchor in nonsense than to put out on the troubled sea of thought.
> — **John Kenneth Galbraith**

normal
noun

1. Being professionally stripped of individuality, uniqueness or distinguishing features.

The weirder you're going to behave, the more normal you should look. It works in reverse, too. When I see a kid with three or four rings in his nose, I know there is absolutely nothing extraordinary about that person.

— P.J. O'Rourke

Everyone seems normal . . . until you get to know them. This includes you.

— Unknown

Normal is getting dressed in clothes that you buy for work and driving through traffic in a car that you are still paying for in order to get to the job you need to pay for the clothes and the car, and the house you leave vacant all day so you can afford to live in it.

— Ellen DeGeneres

A characteristic of the normal child is he doesn't act that way very often.

— Unknown

nose
noun

1. The extreme outpost of the face.

It has been observed that one's nose is never so happy as when thrust into the affairs of others, from which some physiologists have drawn the inference that the nose is devoid of the sense of smell.

— Ambrose Bierce

notoriety
noun

1. The fame of one's competitor.

2. The kind of renown most accessible and acceptable to mediocrity.

novel
noun

1. A species of composition bearing the same relation to literature that the panorama bears to art.

2. A well-padded short story.

Every journalist has a novel in him, which is an excellent place for it.
— **Russel Lynes**

There are three rules for writing the novel. Unfortunately, no one knows what they are.
— **W. Somerset Maugham**

This is not a novel to be tossed aside lightly. It should be thrown aside with great force.
— **Dorothy Parker**

 # (AS IN "OUTCAST")

oath
noun

1. In law, a solemn appeal to the Deity, made binding the penalty for perjury.

A politician under oath is a bit like a tumor under chemotherapy.
— **William Ferraiolo**

oblivion
noun

1. Cold storage for high hopes.
2. A dormitory without an alarm clock.
3. Fame's eternal dumping ground.

obsolete
adjective

1. No longer used by the timid, said chiefly of words.

obstinate
adjective

1. Resistant to truth as advocated by you.

occasional
adjective

1. Afflicting us with unpredictable frequency.

ocean
noun

1. A body of water occupying about two-thirds of a world, made by The Creator for man – who has no gills.

The fact that humans can drown in 2/3 of the world shows God's ultimate plan for us. If global warming is a fact, it shows man's urgent desire to meet his maker.

— **Guy Smith**

offensive
adjective

1. Generating disagreeable emotions or sensations, as does passed gas, the approach of a used car sales person, or the smile of an attorney.

old
adjective

1. Discredited by lapse of time and offensive to the popular taste.

Thirty-five is when you finally get your head together and your body starts falling apart.

— **Unknown**

It is easier to get older than it is to get wiser.

— **Unknown**

The dead might as well try to speak to the living as the old to the young.

— **Willa Cather**

Middle age is when your broad mind and narrow waist begin to change places.

— **E. Joseph Crossman**

The really frightening thing about middle age is that you know you'll grow out of it.

— **Doris Day**

Don't complain about growing old – many people don't have that privilege.

— **Earl Warren**

The young have aspirations that never come to pass, the old have reminiscences of what never happened.

— **H.H. Munro**

I don't mind getting old, given the alternative.

— **Guy Smith**

omen
noun

1. A sign that something will happen if nothing happens.

opera
noun

1. A play representing life in another universe whose inhabitants have no speech but song, no motions but gestures, and no postures but attitudes.

> I don't mind what language an opera is sung in so long as it is a language I don't understand.
> **— Sir Edward Appleton**

operational
adjective

1. An object or process which functions properly by virtue of failing to fulfill any practical purpose.

opiate
noun

1. An unlocked door in the prison of Identity, which leads into the jail yard.

opportunist
noun

1. A person who starts taking a bath when he accidentally falls into a river.

opportunity
noun

1. A favorable occasion for grasping a disappointment.

> The early bird may get the worm, but it's the second mouse that gets the cheese.
> **— Unknown**

Equal opportunity means everyone will have a fair chance at being incompetent.

— **Laurence J. Peter**

Opportunity is missed by most people because it is dressed in overalls and looks like work.

— **Thomas Edison**

oppose
verb

1. To assist an enemy with obstructions and objections.

opposition
noun

1. In politics, the party that prevents the government from running amuck by hamstringing it.

To you I'm an atheist; to God, I'm the Loyal Opposition.

— **Woody Allen**

optimism
noun

1. The doctrine, or belief, that everything is beautiful, including what is ugly, everything good, especially the bad, and everything right that is wrong.

The glass is neither half empty nor half full. It is merely twice as large as it needs to be.

— **Unknown**

I find nothing more depressing than optimism.

— **Paul Fussell**

The place where optimism most flourishes is the lunatic asylum.

— **Havelock Ellis**

The basis of optimism is sheer terror.

— **Oscar Wilde**

[Optimism] is held with greatest tenacity by those most accustomed to the mischance of falling into adversity, and is most acceptably expounded with the grin that apes a smile. Being a blind faith, it is inaccessible to the light of disproof – an intellectual disorder, yielding to no treatment but death. It is hereditary, but fortunately not contagious.

— **Ambrose Bierce**

optimist
noun

1. One who says the glass is half full, but never asks where the other half is.
2. A person who while falling from a cliff declares "See, I am not injured yet."
3. A person with a digestive disorder who is incapable of getting nutrition from reality.
4. A proponent of the doctrine that black is white.
5. A person without experience.

An optimist stays up to see the New Year in. A pessimist waits to make sure the old one leaves.

— **Bill Vaughan**

The optimist proclaims that we live in the best of all possible worlds; and the pessimist fears this is true.

— **Irving Caesar**

oratory
noun

1. A conspiracy between speech and action to defeat understanding.
2. Tyranny tempered by stenography.

originality
noun

1. Process whereby you remember what you heard but forgot where you heard it.

Everything of importance has been said before by somebody who did not discover it.

— **Alfred North Whitehead**

> Don't worry about people stealing an idea. If it's original, you will have to ram it down their throats.
> — **Howard Aiken**

> About the most originality that any writer can hope to achieve honestly is to steal with good judgment.
> — **Josh Billings**

orphan
noun

1. A living person whom death has deprived of the power of filial ingratitude.

orthodox
noun

1. An ox wearing the popular religious yoke.

outcome
noun

1. A particular type of disappointment.

> By the kind of intelligence that sees in an exception a proof of the rule the wisdom of an act is judged by the outcome, the result. This is immortal nonsense; the wisdom of an act is to be judged by the light that the doer had when he performed it.
> — **Ambrose Bierce**

outdo
transitive verb

1. To make an enemy.

outdoors
noun

1. A location used to inspire poets, romantics, and other annoying people.
2. That part of one's universe which government has been unable to collect taxes.
3. A natural repellant for computer programmers.

ovation
noun

1. Humans imitating seals to earn another theatrical or musical fish.

overwork
noun

1. A dangerous disorder affecting public servants who want to go fishing.

oyster
noun

1. A slimy, gobby shellfish which "civilization" gives men the fortitude to eat without first removing its entrails.

> Some people purport that oysters are aphrodisiacs. Nonsense. This is a ruse by men to make certain sexual favors more palatable to women by the virtue of comparison.
>
> — **Guy Smith**

P (AS IN "PESSIMISTIC")

P/E ratio
noun

1. The percentage of investors wetting their pants as the stock market keeps crashing.

pain
noun

1. An uncomfortable frame of mind that may have a physical basis in something that is being done to the body, or maybe purely mental, caused by the good fortune of another.
2. Biological sensations confirming one is alive when they would prefer to not be.

painting
noun

1. The process of protecting flat, canvas surfaces from the weather and exposing them to the critic.

> Rembrandt painted 700 pictures. Of these, 3,000 are still in existence.
> — **Wilhelm Bode**

> Formerly, painting and sculpture were combined in the same work: the ancients painted their statues. The only present alliance between the two arts is that the modern painter chisels his patrons.
> — **Ambrose Bierce**

palace
noun

1. A costly residence reserved for the despots of politics or the despots of commerce.

palm
noun

1. A species of tree having several varieties, of which the familiar "itching palm" (Palma hominis) is most widely distributed and sedulously cultivated. This noble vegetable exudes a kind of invisible gum, which may be detected by applying to the bark a piece of gold or silver. The metal will adhere with remarkable tenacity.

2. An utterly reliable and discreet bordello ably operated by Mother Thumb and her four daughters.

palmistry
noun

1. A popular method of obtaining money by false pretenses.

> [Palistry] consists in "reading character" in the wrinkles made by closing the hand. The pretense is not altogether false; character can really be read very accurately in this way, for the wrinkles in every hand submitted plainly spell the word "dupe."
> — **Ambrose Bierce**

pandemonium
noun

1. Literally, the Place of All the Demons. Most of them have escaped into politics and the place is now used as a lecture hall by socialists.

pantheism
noun

1. The doctrine that everything is God, in contradistinction to the doctrine that God is everything.

pantomime
noun

1. A play in which the story is told without violence to the language.

2. The least disagreeable form of drama, though less humorous than opera.

paranoid
noun

1. Someone who knows only a little of what's going on.

pardon
verb

1. To suspend a penalty and restore one to their life of crime.

2. To amplify the lure of crime by institutionalizing ingratitude.

parenthood
noun

1. Feeding the mouth that bites you.

party
noun

1. In American politics, an article of merchandise purchasable in sets.

> No one party can fool all of the people all of the time. That's why we have two parties.
> **— Bob Hope**
>
> The main purpose of holding children's parties is to remind yourself that there are children more awful than your own.
> **— Unknown**

passport
noun

1. A document which causes distress both by its necessity and by its absence.

2. A document treacherously inflicted upon a citizen going abroad, exposing him as an alien and singling him out for special reprobation.

past
noun

1. That part of Eternity with some small fraction of which we have a slight and regrettable acquaintance.

> To live in the past or in the future may be less satisfying than to live in the present, but it can never be as disillusioning.
> — R. D. Laing

pastime
noun

1. Gentle exercise for intellectual disability.
2. A device for promoting dejection.

patience
noun

1. A form of despair disguised as a virtue.

> You can learn many things from children. How much patience you have, for instance.
> — Franklin P. Adams

> I am extraordinarily patient, provided I get my own way in the end.
> — Margaret Thatcher

> Everything comes to those who wait ... except a cat.
> — Marilyn Peterson

patriot
noun

1. An acute form of political blindness.
2. The dupe of statesmen and the tool of conquerors.

patriotism
noun

1. Combustible rubbish ready to fuel the torch of anyone ambitious to illuminate his name.
2. The willingness to kill and be killed for trivial reasons.
3. Arbitrary veneration of real estate above principles.
4. A conviction that one country is superior to all other countries because you were born in it.
5. The last resort of a political scoundrel.

In the United States, doing good has come to be, like patriotism, a favorite device of persons with something to sell.
— **H.L. Mencken**

peace
noun

1. A period of cheating between two periods of fighting. Applicable to affairs international, domestic, and suburban.

I can forgive Alfred Nobel for having invented dynamite, but only a fiend in human form could have invented the Nobel Prize.
— **George Bernard Shaw**

Blessed are the peacemakers, for they shall catch hell from both sides.
— **Burke Marshall (attributed)**

If man does find the solution for world peace it will be the most revolutionary reversal of his record we have ever known.
— **George C. Marshall**

The most menacing political condition is a period of international amity. The student of history who has not been taught to expect the unexpected may justly boast himself inaccessible to the light. "In time of peace prepare for war" has a deeper meaning than is commonly discerned; it means, not merely that all things earthly have an end – that change is the one immutable and eternal law – but that the soil of peace is thickly sown with the seeds of war and singularly suited to their germination and growth.
— **Ambrose Bierce**

pedestrian
noun

1. The variable and often audible part of the roadway, typically under an automobile.

pedigree
noun

1. The known part of the route from an arboreal ancestor with a tail to a suburban descendant with a mortgage.

penis
noun

1. The primary organ that controls all human male higher mental functions, from emotions, to social interactions, to thermonuclear warfare.

Man is living proof that God has a sense humor – he gave him two heads and only enough blood to think with one at a time.
— **Robin Williams**

Any woman who thinks the way to a man's heart is through his stomach is aiming about 10 inches too high.
— **Adrienne E. Gusoff**

penitent
adjective

1. Undergoing or awaiting punishment.

people
noun

1. The most highly evolved of animals that display the most poorly evolved forms of behavior.

The good people sleep much better at night than the bad people. Of course, the bad people enjoy the waking hours much more.
— **Woody Allen**

Everyone is as God has made him, and oftentimes a great deal worse.
— **Miguel de Cervantes**

Actors are the opposite of people.
— **Tom Stoppard**

Great people talk about ideas, average people talk about things, and small people talk about wine.
— **Fran Lebowitz**

People shouldn't be treated like objects. They aren't that valuable.
— **P.J. O'Rourke**

To predict the behavior of ordinary people in advance, you only have to assume that they will always try to escape a disagreeable situation with the smallest possible expenditure of intelligence.
— **Friedrich Nietzsche**

percussive maintenance
noun

1. The art of beating the crap out of equipment in the hope it will start to work. Disturbingly successful.

perfection
noun

1. An imaginary state of quality distinguished from reality by the sentimentality of the viewer.

Have no fear of perfection – you'll never reach it.
— **Salvador Dali**

All parents see their children as perfect, at least until the teen years. This delusion is God's system for keeping parents from selling the little vermin off for medical experimentation.
— **Guy Smith**

perseverance
noun

1. A low virtue where mediocrity achieves an inglorious success.

pessimism
noun

1. A gloomy disposition developed through the disheartening prevalence of optimists and their unsightly smiles.

The glass is neither half empty nor half full. It is merely twice as large as it needs to be.
— **Unknown**

My pessimism extends to the point of even suspecting the sincerity of the pessimists.
— **Jean Rostand**

pessimist
noun

1. An optimist with experience.
2. A person who looks both ways before crossing a one-way street.

> An optimist stays up to see the New Year in. A pessimist waits to make sure the old one leaves.
> — **Bill Vaughan**

> Nobody kills a great idea faster than a bored pessimist.
> — **Unknown**

> Borrow money from pessimists – they don't expect it back.
> — **Steven Wright**

> The optimist proclaims that we live in the best of all possible worlds; and the pessimist fears this is true.
> — **Irving Caesar**

pharmacist
noun

1. The physician's accomplice, the undertaker's benefactor, and the worms provider.

philanthropist
noun

1. A rich (and usually bald) old gentleman who has trained himself to grin while his conscience is picking his pocket.

philistine
noun

1. A person with low tastes, such as an opera enthusiast.
2. A person not blessed with your bigotries.

philosopher
noun

1. A fool who torments himself during life, to be spoken of when dead.

There is only one thing a philosopher can be relied upon to do, and that is to contradict other philosophers.
— **William James**

By all means marry; if you get a good wife, you'll be happy. If you get a bad one, you'll become a philosopher.
— **Socrates**

philosophy
noun

1. A route of many roads leading from nowhere to nothing.

2. Intellectual masturbation.

The point of philosophy is to start with something so simple as not to seem worth stating, and to end with something so paradoxical that no one will believe it.
— **Bertrand Russell**

photograph
noun

1. Artistic representations without the benefit of hiding or exaggerating flaws.

Photographs show people as they really are, which is why nobody likes their own.
— **Guy Smith**

phrenology
noun

1. The science of picking the pocket through the scalp.

physician
noun

1. One upon whom we set our hopes when ill and complaints when well.

physiognomy
noun

1. The art of determining a person's character by the resemblances and differences between his face and our own, which is the natural standard of excellence.

piano
noun

1. A utensil for subduing impenitent visitors. It is operated by depressing the keys of the machine and the spirits of the audience.

picture
noun

1. A representation in two dimensions of something wearisome in three.

pie
noun

1. An advance agent of indigestion.

piety
noun

1. Reverence for the Supreme Being, based upon His supposed resemblance to man.

pig
noun

1. An animal closely allied to the human race by the splendor and vivacity of its appetite.

pillory
noun

1. A mechanical device for inflicting personal distinction – a prototype of the Internet.

piracy
noun

1. Commerce without distraction (see Taxation).

pirate
noun

1. A politician of the high seas.

pitiful
adjective

1. The state of an enemy after an imaginary encounter with oneself.

> Pity the meek, for they shall inherit the earth.
> — **Don Marquis**

plagiarism
noun

1. A literary coincidence followed with an honorable excuse.

> I don't like composers who think. It gets in the way of their plagiarism.
> — **Howard Dietz**

plagiarize
noun

1. To take the thought or style of another writer whom one has never, never read.

plague
noun

1. A punishment of innocent people for mood swings of their God.

plan
transitive verb

1. To bother about the best method of accomplishing an accidental result.

platitude
noun

1. All that remains of a departed truth.
2. The fundamental element of popular literature.
3. A moral without a fable.
4. The wisdom of a million fools in the diction of a dullard.
5. A fossil sentiment in artificial rock.
6. An idea that (a) is admitted to be true by everyone, and (b) that is not true.
7. A thought that snores in words that smoke.

platonic
adjective

1. A relationship unworthy of investment due to the certainty of no profit.

> Platonic Love is a fool's name for the affection between a disability and a frost.
> — **Ambrose Bierce**

please
verb

1. To lay a foundation for imposition.

plot
noun

1. Evil methods employed by one's opponents in baffling one's open and honorable efforts to do the wrong thing.

> As you journey through life take a minute every now and then to give a thought for the other fellow. He could be plotting something.
> — **Dik Browne**

plow
noun

1. An implement that cries for hands accustomed to the pen.

> Those who beat their swords into plowshares will plow for those who don't.
>
> **— Unknown**

plunder
verb

1. To effect a change of ownership with the subtlety of a brass band.

2. To take the property of another without observing the decent and customary reticences of theft.

PMS
noun

1. Pity Me Syndrome
2. Potential Mother of Satan
3. Pass My Shotgun
4. Psychotic Mood Shift
5. Piss and Moan Syndrome
6. Plainly; Men Suck
7. Puffy, Moody and Starving
8. Please My Stomach
9. Provide Me with Sweets
10. Puffy Mid Section

pocket
noun

1. The cradle of motive and the grave of conscience.

2. A target painted for the politician.

poetry
noun

1. A lyrical, literary style calculated to annoy and offend everyone except the poet.

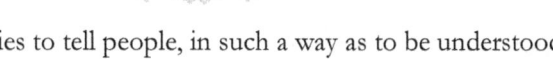

> In science one tries to tell people, in such a way as to be understood by everyone, something that no one ever knew before. But in poetry, it's the exact opposite.
>
> **— Paul Dirac**

police
noun

1. An armed force for protection from, and participation in crime.

> The best car safety device is a rear-view mirror with a cop in it.
> — **Dudley Moore**

> Only high-school wimps and teenage bullies become cops ... and for the very same reason.
> — **Dave C. Milligan**

> We live in an age when pizza gets to your home before the police.
> — **Jeff Marder**

politeness
noun

1. The most acceptable hypocrisy.

political correctness
noun

1. The ideological belief that one can pick up a turd by the clean end.

political science
noun

1. The learning of more and more, about less and less, until one knows nothing at all.

politician
noun

1. One who shakes your hand before elections and your confidence thereafter.
2. An elected official who makes laws for the primary purpose of campaigning against in the next election.
3. Profession held by intellectual prostitutes.
4. An eel in the fundamental mud upon which organized society is erected.

Probably the most distinctive characteristic of the successful politician is selective cowardice.
— **Richard Harris**

Politicians and diapers both need to be changed often, and for the same reason.
— **Bumper Sticker**

Is a politician boinking a prostitute redundant, or a quid pro quo?
— **Guy Smith**

It is fast approaching the point where I don't want to elect anyone stupid enough to want the job.
— **Erma Bombeck**

Aristotle believed that the brain existed merely to cool blood and was not involved in with thinking, which has proven true for certain persons, mainly politicians.
— **Derived from Will Cuppy**

What this country needs are more unemployed politicians.
— **Edward Langley**

The only time two men should ever be in bed together is if one is a lobbyist and one is a politician.
— **Jay Leno**

Today, wanting someone else's money is called "need", wanting to keep your own money is called "greed", and "compassion" is when politicians arrange the transfer.
— **Joseph Sobran**

My concerns with churches meddling in political affairs have nothing to do with faith based morality rubbing off on politicians. The concern is that the Churches will find themselves adopting the relative morality associated with politics.
— **Kenneth Corbin**

I have always felt that a politician is to be judged by the animosities he excites among his opponents.
— **Winston Churchill**

Instead of giving a politician the keys to the city, it might be better to change the locks.
— **Doug Larson**

It is dangerous for a national candidate to say things that people might remember.
— **Eugene McCarthy**

An honest politician is one who, when he is bought, will stay bought.

— **Simon Cameron**

Now I know what a statesman is; he's a dead politician. We need more statesmen.

— **Bob Edwards**

Politicians are the same all over. They promise to build a bridge even where there is no river.

— **Nikita Khrushchev**

The reason there are so few female politicians is that it is too much trouble to put makeup on two faces.

— **Maureen Murphy**

Ninety percent of the politicians give the other ten percent a bad reputation.

— **Henry Kissinger**

When the politicians complain that TV turns the proceedings into a circus, it should be made clear that the circus was already there, and that TV has merely demonstrated that not all the performers are well trained.

— **Edward R. Murrow**

I have come to the conclusion that politics are too serious a matter to be left to the politicians.

— **Charles De Gaulle**

A recent survey was said to prove that the people we Americans most admire are our politicians and doctors. I don't believe it. They are simply the people we are most afraid of. And with the most reason.

— **Unknown**

Ninety-eight percent of the adults in this country are decent, hard-working, honest Americans. It's the other lousy two percent that get all the publicity. But then – we elected them.

— **Lily Tomlin**

A politician under oath is a bit like a tumor under chemotherapy.

— **William Ferraiolo**

An honest politician appears on the scene as often as a celibate whore.

— **William Ferraiolo**

politics
noun

1. The gentle art of getting votes from the poor and campaign funds from the rich, by promising to protect each from the other.
2. The conduct of public affairs for private advantage.
3. The skilled use of blunt objects.
4. A strife of interests masquerading as a contest of principles.
5. The process of choosing between the disastrous and the unpalatable.
6. The art of looking for trouble, finding it whether it exists or not, diagnosing it incorrectly, and applying the wrong remedy.

In politics, absurdity is not a handicap.
— **Napoleon Bonaparte**

The end move in politics is always to pick up a gun.
— **Richard Buckminster Fuller**

Too bad the only people who know how to run the country are busy driving cabs and cutting hair.
— **George Burn**

Politics is my second favorite contact sport, right after sex. With either, I know I'm getting screwed.
— **Guy Smith**

Politics is not a bad profession. If you succeed there are many rewards, if you disgrace yourself you can always write a book.
— **Ronald Reagan**

In politics, if you want anything said, ask a man – if you want anything done, ask a woman.
— **Margaret Thatcher**

We need anything politically important rationed out like Pez: small, sweet, and coming out of a funny, plastic head.
— **Dennis Miller**

You know what's interesting about Washington? It's the kind of place where second-guessing has become second nature.
— **George W. Bush**

Nothing can so alienate a voter from the political system as backing a winning candidate.

— Mark B. Cohen

Politics is perhaps the only profession for which no preparation is thought necessary.
— Robert Louis Stevenson

Crime does not pay ... as well as politics.
— Alfred E. Newman

Politics is the art of preventing people from taking part in affairs which properly concern them.
— Paul Valery

Politics is supposed to be the second oldest profession. I have come to realize that it bears a very close resemblance to the first.
— Ronald Reagan

I have come to the conclusion that politics are too serious a matter to be left to the politicians.
— Charles De Gaulle

The etymology of the word "politics" is instructive. The prefix comes from the Greek "poly", meaning "many" and "tics" is from Latin for "blood sucking parasites". Thus, "many blood sucking parasites" as exemplified by congress.
— Unknown

Being in politics is like being a football coach. You have to be smart enough to understand the game, and dumb enough to think it's important.
— Eugene McCarthy

polygamy
noun

1. A house of atonement fitted with several stools of repentance, as distinguished from monogamy, which has but one.

Polygamy shows the dysfunction of monogamy. A man wants a different woman in his bed every night. A woman can barely stand the same man in her bed once a week.
— Guy Smith

The criminal penalty for polygamy is two wives.
— Unknown

portable
adjective

1. Exposed to mutable ownership.

positive
adjective

1. Mistaken at the top of one's voice.

positivism
noun

1. A philosophy that denies our knowledge of reality and affirms our ignorance of the apparent.

posterity
noun

1. An appellate court which reverses the judgment of one's contemporaries.

poverty
noun

1. A file provided for the teeth of the rats of socialism.

> I think that's how Chicago got started. A bunch of people in New York said, Gee, I'm enjoying the crime and the poverty here, but it just isn't cold enough. Let's go west.
> **— Richard Jeni**

> The number of plans for [poverty's] abolition equals that of the reformers who suffer from it, plus that of the philosophers who know nothing about it. Its victims are distinguished by possession of all the virtues and by their faith in leaders seeking to conduct them into a prosperity where they believe these to be unknown.
> **— Ambrose Bierce**

power
noun

1. The only narcotic regulated by the SEC instead of the FDA.

The Devil's Dictionary

Knowledge is power. Power corrupts. Study Hard. Be evil.
— **Unknown**

Giving money and power to government is like giving whiskey and car keys to teenage boys.
— **P.J. O'Rourke**

CNN is one of the participants in the war. I have a fantasy where Ted Turner is elected president but refuses because he doesn't want to give up power.
— **Arthur C. Clarke**

It is said that power corrupts, but actually it's more true that power attracts the corruptible. The sane are usually attracted by other things than power.
— **David Brin**

Nearly all men can stand adversity, but if you want to test a man's character, give him power.
— **Abraham Lincoln**

Power corrupts. Absolute power is kind of neat.
— **John Lehman, Secretary of the Navy, 1981-1987**

Some men manage not to be corrupted by power. This is almost a shame.
— **William Ferraiolo**

Absolute power corrupts absolutely. What does this say about God?
— **Guy Smith**

pray
noun

1. Wishing aloud for things you know will not happen.

verb

2. To ask that the laws of the universe be annulled on behalf of a single petitioner who is confessedly unworthy.

preaching
noun

1. The science of adapting sermons to the spiritual needs, capacities, and bigotries of the congregation.

precedent
noun

1. In law, a previous decision, rule or practice which, in the absence of a definite statute, has whatever force and authority a judge may choose to give it, thereby greatly simplifying his task of doing as he pleases.

predicament
noun

1. The result of consistency.

predilection
noun

1. The preparatory stage of disillusion.

preexistence
noun

1. Time wasted before cocktail hour.
2. An unnoted factor in Creation.

preference
noun

1. A sentiment, or frame of mind, induced by the erroneous belief that one thing is better than another.

prehistoric
adjective

1. Antedating the art and practice of perpetuating falsehood.

prejudice
noun

1. A vagrant opinion without visible means of support.

> Without the aid of prejudice and custom I should not be able to find my way across the room.
>
> **— William Hazlitt**

> I am free of all prejudice. I hate everyone equally.
> — W.C. Fields

> Nobody outside of a baby carriage or a judge's chamber believes in an unprejudiced point of view.
> — Lillian Hellman

> If we were to wake up some morning and find that everyone was the same race, creed and color, we would find some other cause for prejudice by noon.
> — George Aiken

prerogative
noun

1. A sovereign's right to do wrong.

prescription
noun

1. A receipt for a medical product which was not wanted, does not work and cannot be returned.
2. A physician's guess at what will best prolong an ailment with the least harm to the patient.

present
noun

1. That part of eternity that divides the domain of disappointment from the realm of hope.

> To live in the past or in the future may be less satisfying than to live in the present, but it can never be as disillusioning.
> — R. D. Laing

presentable
adjective

1. Hideously appareled for specific manners, times and places.

All God's children are not beautiful. Most of God's children are, in fact, barely presentable.

— **Fran Lebowitz**

preside
verb

1. To guide the action of a deliberative body to an undesirable result.

presidency
noun

1. The greased pig in the field game of American politics.

Anybody who wants the presidency so much that he'll spend two years organizing and campaigning for it is not to be trusted with the office.

— **David Broder**

president
noun

1. In American politics, the Liar in Chief.

When I was a boy I was told that anybody could become President. Now I'm beginning to believe it.

— **Clarence Darrow**

In our brief national history we have shot four of our presidents, worried five of them to death, impeached [two] and hounded another out of office. And when all else fails, we hold an election and assassinate their character.

— **P.J. O'Rourke**

Anyone who is capable of getting themselves made President should on no account be allowed to do the job.

— **Douglas Adams**

Americans have different ways of saying things. They say "elevator", we say "lift" ... they say "President", we say "stupid psychopathic git".

— **Alexi Sayle**

> In America any boy may become President and I suppose it's just one of the risks he takes.
> — **Adlai E. Stevenson Jr.**

> As democracy is perfected, the [presidency] represents, more and more closely, the inner soul of the people. We move toward a lofty ideal. On some great and glorious day the plain folks of the land will reach their heart's desire at last, and the White House will be adorned by a downright moron.
> — **H. L. Mencken**

prevaricator
noun

1. A liar in the larval state.

2. An apprentice politician.

price
noun

1. Fair value, plus a premium for the wear and tear of one's conscience in demanding it.

primate
noun

1. The head of a church who disavows the process of evolution from other primates.

prison
noun

1. A place of reward for political and personal service.

2. A place of punishments and rewards for criminals both desirable and political.

> There is never enough time, unless you're serving it.
> — **Malcolm Forbes**

private

adjective

1. That which when displayed openly is ignored, and when concealed is exposed.

noun

2. Battlefield fertilizer.

3. A military gentleman with a field marshal's baton in his knapsack and an impediment in his hope.

---

problem

noun

1. Your name for my issue.

> Each success only buys an admission ticket to a more difficult problem.
> — **Henry Kissinger**

> An undefined problem has an infinite number of solutions.
> — **Robert A. Humphrey**

> It may be true that the law cannot make a man love me, but it can stop him from lynching me, and I think that's pretty important.
> — **Martin Luther King Jr.**

> I have yet to see any problem, however complicated, which, when you looked at it in the right way, did not become still more complicated.
> — **Poul Anderson**

> No problem is so formidable that you can't walk away from it.
> — **Charles M. Schulz**

---

procrastination

verb

1. The art of keeping up with yesterday.

2. The belief that anything worth doing would have been done already.

Never put off until tomorrow what you can do the day after tomorrow.

— **Mark Twain**

programming
verb

1. *Computers* To engage in a pastime similar to banging one's head against a wall, but with fewer opportunities for reward.

Programming today is a race between software engineers striving to build bigger and better idiot-proof programs, and the Universe trying to produce bigger and better idiots. So far, the Universe is winning.

— **Rich Cook**

The first 90 percent of the code accounts for the first 90 percent of the development time? The remaining 10 percent of the code accounts for the other 90 percent of the development time.

— **Tom Cargill**

progress
noun

1. The process through which the Internet has evolved from smart people in front of dumb terminals to dumb people in front of smart terminals.
2. The exchange of one nuisance for another nuisance.

The chief obstacle to the progress of the human race is the human race.

— **Don Marquis**

Unquestionably, there is progress. The average American now pays out twice as much in taxes as he formerly got in wages.

— **H.L. Mencken**

All progress is based upon a universal innate desire on the part of every organism to live beyond its income.

— **Samuel Butler**

Progress might have been all right once, but it has gone on too long.

— **Ogden Nash**

> Progress isn't made by early risers. It's made by lazy men trying to find easier ways to do something.
> — **Robert Heinlein**

proof
noun

1. Evidence having a shade more of plausibility than of unlikelihood.

2. The testimony of two credible liars as opposed to that of only one.

> Science has proof without any certainty. Creationists have certainty without any proof.
> — **Ashley Montague**

property
noun

1. Whatever gratifies the passion for possession in one and disappoints it in all others.

> No man's life, liberty or property are safe while the legislature is in session.
> — **Judge Gideon J. Tucker**

prophecy
noun

1. The art and practice of selling one's credibility for future delivery.

proselytize
verb

1. To annoy heretics with one's own religious heresy.

prospect
noun

1. An expectation, usually forbidden.

2. An outlook, usually forbidding.

prototype
noun

1. First stage in the life cycle of a computer product, followed by pre-alpha, alpha, beta, release version, corrected release version, upgrade, corrected upgrade, etc. Unlike its successors, the prototype is not expected to work.

providential
adjective

1. Unexpectedly and conspicuously beneficial to the person so describing it.

prude
noun

1. A bawdy babe hiding behind her demeanor.

psychiatrist
noun

1. A professional who asks you a lot of expensive questions that your spouse asks for free.

> Two out of three psychiatrists surveyed think the third one is nuts.
> — **Mario Di Boscio**

psychiatry
noun

1. A therapeutic process whereby people correct their faults by disclosing their parents' shortcomings.

> Television has done much for psychiatry by spreading information about it, as well as contributing to the need for it.
> — **Alfred Hitchcock**

publish
noun

1. In literary affairs, to happily become victuals for critics.

Punctuality
adjective

1. The virtue of the bored.

> I have noticed that the people who are late are often so much jollier than the people who have to wait for them.
> — **E. V. Lucas**

> The trouble with being punctual is that nobody's there to appreciate it.
> — **Franklin P. Jones**

puritanism
noun

1. The haunting fear that someone, somewhere, may be happy.

 (AS IN "QUIT WHILE YOU ARE ...")

queen
noun

1. A woman by whom the realm is ruled when there is a king, and through whom it is ruled when there is not.

quill
noun

1. An implement of torture yielded by a goose and commonly wielded by an ass.

> This use of the quill is now obsolete, but its modern equivalent, the steel pen, is wielded by the same everlasting Presence.
> — **Ambrose Bierce**

quiver
noun

1. A portable sheath in which ancient statesmen and aboriginal lawyers carried their lighter arguments.

quorum
noun

1. A sufficient number of members of a deliberative body to have their own way.

> In the United States Senate a quorum consists of the chairman of the Committee on Finance and a messenger from the White House; in the House of Representatives, of the Speaker and the devil.
> — **Ambrose Bierce**

quotation
noun

1. The act of repeating erroneously the words of another.
2. A dullards version of creative thinking.

The ability to quote is a serviceable substitute for wit.
— **W. Somerset Maugham**

The point of quotations is that one can use another's words to be insulting.
— **Amanda Cross**

# (AS IN "RIDICULOUS")

rabble
noun

1. In a republic, those who exercise a supreme authority tempered by fraudulent elections.

> The rabble is like the sacred Simurgh, of Arabian fable – omnipotent on condition that it do nothing.
> **— Ambrose Bierce**

rack
noun

1. An argumentative implement of the Inquisition, used in persuading devotees of a false faith to embrace the living truth.

radicalism
noun

1. The conservatism of tomorrow injected into the affairs of today.

ramshackle
adjective

1. Pertaining to a certain order of architecture, otherwise known as the Normal American.

> Most of the public buildings of the United States are of the Ramshackle order, though some of our earlier architects preferred the Ironic.
> **— Ambrose Bierce**

rank
noun

1. In military organizations, the inverse representation of intelligence.
2. Relative elevation in the scale of human worth.

> Language can be very instructive based on the commonality of meaning of certain word. Take the word "rank". In one sense it represents the hierarchy of status for humans. It also means smelly or odiferous. We routinely observe that people of higher rank become more rank, thus confirming the shared origin of the word.
> — Guy Smith

ransom
noun

1. The most unprofitable of investments.

rapacity
noun

1. The thrift of power.
2. Providence without industry.

rapper
noun

1. An urban redneck.

rascal
noun

1. A fool with a good PR agent.

rash
adjective

1. Insensible to the value of your advice.

rational
adjective

1. Devoid of all delusions save those of observation, experience, and reflection.

It has been said that man is a rational animal. All my life I have been searching for evidence which could support this.
— **Bertrand Russell**

Man is a rational animal who always loses his temper when called upon to act in accordance with the dictates of reason.
— **Orson Welles**

rattlesnake
noun

1. The closest evolutionary ancestor of the trial lawyer.

razor
noun

1. A lethal weapon wielded by a man across his throat and a woman across her leg. It has been the source of much bloodshed.

reach
noun

1. The radius of action of the human hand. In politics, the reach is limited to the taxpayers pocket.

reading
noun

1. The general body of what one reads. In America, it consists primarily of romance novels, sports pages, and the flotsam of the Internet.

When I read about the evils of drinking, I gave up reading.
— **Henny Youngman**

reality

noun

1. The dream of a mad philosopher.
2. That which, when you stop believing in it, doesn't go away.
3. Something to rise above.

> Punching your fist on a concrete wall gains you deep insight into the true nature of the universe.
> — **Unknown**
>
> Why watch reality TV in a TV based reality?
> — **RayB**
>
> Imagination is the one weapon in the war against reality.
> — **Jules de Gaultier**
>
> Reality is merely an illusion, albeit a very persistent one.
> — **Albert Einstein**
>
> Reality is the leading cause of stress amongst those in touch with it.
> — **Jane Wagner**
>
> Reality is nothing but a collective hunch.
> — **Lily Tomlin**

rear

noun

1. In American military matters, that exposed part of the army that is rightfully nearest Congress.

reason

noun

1. The poor cousin in the otherwise proud families of Logic and Critical Thinking.
2. The precursor to prejudice.

> I prefer the company of peasants because they have not been educated sufficiently to reason incorrectly.
> — **Michel de Montaigne**

> Man is a rational animal who always loses his temper when called upon to act in accordance with the dictates of reason.
> — **Orson Welles**

reasonable
adjective

1. Hospitable to persuasion, dissuasion, and evasion.

2. Accessible to the infection of our own opinions.

> The reasonable man adapts himself to the world; the unreasonable one persists in trying to adapt the world to himself. Therefore all progress depends on the unreasonable man.
> — **George Bernard Shaw**

rebel
noun

1. A proponent of a new misrule who has failed to establish it.

> The young always have the same problem – how to rebel and conform at the same time. They have now solved this by defying their parents and copying one another.
> — **George Chapman**

recession
noun

1. A momentary lapse in greed.

> It's a recession when your neighbor loses his job; it's a depression when you lose your own.
> — **Harry S Truman**

recollect
verb

1. To recall with new additions something that was not previously known.

reconciliation
noun

1. A suspension of hostilities.

2. An armed truce for the purpose of digging up the dead.

reconsider
verb

1. To prepare to make the incorrect decision after all.

2. To seek justification for a decision already made.

recount
noun

1. In American politics, another throw of the dice. A gift provided to the player against whom the dice are loaded.

> When a man named Daley from Chicago gets off an airplane and says "I'm here to help you count your ballots", it is time to load your shotgun. (uttered during the Florida presidential recount of 2000)
> — **Guy Smith**

recreation
noun

1. A particular kind of dejection to relieve general fatigue.

recruit
noun

1. A person distinguishable from a civilian by his uniform, and distinguishable from a soldier by his gait.

rectitude
noun

1. The formal, dignified bearing adopted by proctologists.

redemption
noun

1. Deliverance of sinners from the penalty of their sin; in Christianity through their murder of the deity against whom they sinned.

redress
noun

1. Reparations without satisfaction.

referendum
noun

1. A question which has been answered before being asked.

2. A proposed legislation put to a popular vote in order to learn the consensus of public opinion.

reflection
noun

1. An action of the mind whereby we obtain a clearer view of our relationship to yesterday, and are able to avoid perils that we shall not again encounter.

refusal
noun

1. Denial of something desired, such as the execution of a lawyer by his client.

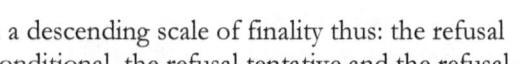

> Refusals are graded in a descending scale of finality thus: the refusal absolute, the refusal conditional, the refusal tentative and the refusal feminine. The last is called by some casuists the refusal assentive.
> **— Ambrose Bierce**

reincarnation
noun

1. A spiritual belief that we live multiple lives, one after the next, in order to successfully make every possible mistake.

religion
noun

1. Mythology collected to establish the social discipline of your neighbor.

2. Original commerce.

3. Man's attempt to explain God, much to God's annoyance.

4. A theological fungus that thrives best in the dark and when fed by bullshit.

5. A daughter of Hope and Fear, used to explain to Ignorance the nature of the Unknowable.

One man's God often is another man's abomination.
— **Unknown**

Religion fails from the start, by trying to conceive of God, who by definition is inconceivable.
— **Guy Smith**

A stupid man's report of what a clever man says can never be accurate, because he unconsciously translates what he hears into something he can understand. [Editor: This explains prophets and their relationship to God, and the acolyte's relationship to the prophet]
— **Bertrand Russell**

With or without religion, you would have good people doing good things and evil people doing evil things. But for good people to do evil things, that takes religion.
— **Steven Weinberg**

My theology, briefly, is that the universe was dictated but not signed.
— **Christopher Morley**

The more I study religions the more I am convinced that man never worshipped anything but himself.
— **Sir Richard Francis Burton**

The fact that a believer is happier than a skeptic is no more to the point than the fact than a drunken man is happier than a sober one.
— **George Bernard Shaw**

One man's theology is another man's belly laugh.
— **Robert Heinlein**

Faith may be defined briefly as an illogical belief in the occurrence of the improbable.
— **H. L. Mencken**

> People who insist that God is everywhere are usually the same people trying to corral us into churches, mosques and synagogues.
> — **William Ferraiolo**

> Absolute faith corrupts as absolutely as absolute power.
> — **Eric Hoffer**

> Say what you will about the Ten Commandments, you must always come back to the pleasant fact that there are only ten of them.
> — **H. L. Mencken**

reliquary
noun

1. A receptacle for such sacred objects such as pieces of the true cross, short ribs of saints or a meteor shard from Alpha Centari.

renown
noun

1. A degree of distinction somewhere between notoriety and fame – a little more supportable than the former and a little more intolerable than the latter.

reparation
noun

1. Financial penance for a wrong, deducted from the profit in committing said wrong.

repartee
noun

1. Prudent insult in retort.
2. Retribution practiced by gentlemen who have an aversion to violence, but a strong disposition to offend.

repentance
noun

1. A plea bargain for sin.
2. The faithful attendant and follower of Punishment.

reporter
noun

1. A writer who guesses at the truth and then dispels the truth with a tempest of words.

2. A scribe for newspapers and television who gathers facts before reporting his opinion.

> The one function TV news performs very well is that when there is no news we give it to you with the same emphasis as if there were.
> — **David Brinkley**

> So talking about a liberal slant to [the media] is a little like talking to a fish about water. The fish says, "Water? What's water?" It's just what we swim in.
> — **John Stossel**

> Trying to be a first-rate reporter on the average American newspaper is like trying to play Bach's *St. Matthew's Passion* on a ukulele.
> — **Bagdikian's Observation**

> I believe in equality for everyone, except reporters and photographers.
> — **Mahatma Gandhi**

representative
noun

1. In national politics, a member of the Lower House in this world, who has no hope of promotion in the next.

2. A member of Congress whose job it is to misrepresent the will of their constituents.

> Democracy is "representative" in roughly the same sense that the Roman Empire was "Holly".
> — **William Ferraiolo**

reprobation
noun

1. theology: the state of a prenatal, damned mortal.

The doctrine of reprobation was taught by Calvin, whose joy in it was somewhat marred by the sad sincerity of his conviction that although some are foredoomed to perdition, others are predestined to salvation.

— **Ambrose Bierce**

republic
noun

1. The form of government practiced in America by which the people elect representatives they distrust, to create laws they despise, for the country they love.
2. A form of government whereby the thing governing and the thing governed are the same, and thus there is only a permitted authority to enforce an optional obedience.
3. Democracy by proxy – organized mob rule.

In a republic, the foundation of public order is the ever lessening habit of submission inherited from ancestors who, being truly governed, submitted because they had to. There are as many kinds of republics as there are graduations between the despotism whence they came and the anarchy whither they lead.

— **Ambrose Bierce**

resentment
noun

1. Taking poison and waiting for the other person to die.

resident
adjective

1. Unable to leave.

resign
transitive verb

1. politics: a skillful tactic for avoiding impeachment, prosecution, tar, and feathers.
2. To renounce an advantage for a greater advantage.

resolute
adjective

1. Obstinate in a course that we approve.

2. The most annoying posture an enemy can maintain.

respectability
noun

1. The union of a liaison between a bald head and a bank account.

2. What the businessman craves, the gold digger is denied, the politician can never attain, and the prostitute believes is over rated.

respirator
noun

1. An apparatus fitted over the nose and mouth of an inhabitant of Los Angeles, to filter the visible universe on its passage to the lungs.

respite
noun

1. A suspension of prosecution against a sentenced assassin, allowing authorities to determine if the murder may not have been committed by the prosecuting attorney.

2. Any break in the continuity of a disagreeable expectation.

respond
intransitive verb

1. To annoy a partner in conversation by disrupting monologue.

responsibility
noun

1. A detachable burden easily shifted to the shoulders of God, Fate, Fortune, Luck, or one's neighbor.

> Liberty means responsibility. That is why most men dread it.
> — George Barnard Shaw

The government is like a baby's alimentary canal, with a happy appetite at one end and no responsibility at the other.

— **Ronald Reagan**

restitution
noun

1. Payment to compensate for a crime or sin. Restitution is made in cash when one is convicted in court, and through endowments to universities, libraries, and orphanages when one in convicted by conscious.

retaliation
noun

1. The foundation of the house of Law, both primitive and civilized.

retribution
noun

1. A rain of fire-and-brimstone that falls upon the just, and upon the unjust who have not procured shelter by evicting the former.

reveille
noun

1. A signal to sleeping soldiers to cease dreaming of battlefields, and to enter them instead.

Revelation
noun

1. A famous book in which St. John the Divine concealed all that he knew. The revealing is done by commentators, who know nothing.

reverence
noun

1. The spiritual attitude of a man to a god, and a dog to a man, and a flea to a dog. For each, their reverence is driven mainly by hunger.

revolution
noun

1. In American history, the substitution of the rule of an Administration for that of a Ministry, whereby the welfare and happiness of the people were advanced a full half-inch.
2. politics: an abrupt change in the form of misgovernment.

> The most radical revolutionary will become a conservative the day after the revolution.
> — **Hannah Arendt**

> Revolutions are usually accompanied by a considerable effusion of blood, but are accounted worth it – this appraisement being made by beneficiaries whose blood had not the mischance to be shed. The French revolution is of incalculable value to the Socialist of today; when he pulls the string actuating its bones its gestures are inexpressibly terrifying to gory tyrants suspected of fomenting law and order.
> — **Ambrose Bierce**

rhyme
noun

1. Agreeing yet disagreeable sounds in the terminals of verse.

ribaldry
noun

1. Censorious language by another concerning oneself.

rich
adjective

1. According to Socialist doctrine, the holding in trust of the property of the indolent, the incompetent, the unthrifty, the envious, and the luckless. This definition has been discounted by the sane.

> If all the rich people in the world divided up their money among themselves there wouldn't be enough to go around.
> — **Christina Stead**

It is the wretchedness of being rich that you have to live with rich people.
— **Logan Pearsall Smith**

If work were such a splendid thing the rich would have kept more of it for themselves.
— **Bruce Grocott**

Who is rich? He that is content. Who is that? Nobody.
— **Benjamin Franklin**

When a man tells you that he got rich through hard work, ask him "Whose?"
— **Don Marquis**

The tone of voice used is the same when somebody says "tax the rich" or "burn the Jews."
— **Ralph Seifert**

ridicule
noun

1. Words designed to show that the person for whom they are uttered is devoid of the dignity distinguishing he who utters them.

right
noun

1. Legitimate authority to be, to have, or to do as one pleases; as the right to be a king, the right to do one's neighbor, the right to a taxpayer assistance, etc.

    Sometimes what's right isn't as important as what's profitable.
    — **Trey Parker and Matt Stone**

    It is dangerous to be right when the government is wrong.
    — **Voltaire**

    Always do right. This will gratify some people and astonish the rest.
    — **Mark Twain**

riot
noun

1. A popular form of entertainment given to the police by innocent bystanders.

rite
noun

1. A ceremony fixed by law, precept, or custom, with all traces of sincerity carefully squeezed out of it.

ritualism
noun

1. A garden in which God can walk with perfect freedom, providing he keeps off the grass.

road
noun

1. A device of religious significance to Americans, aside from pedestrians and other atheists.

2. A path along which one may pass from where it is too tiresome to be to where it is too futile to go.

robber
noun

1. A candid man of affairs.

> It is related of Voltaire that one night he and some traveling companion lodged at a wayside inn. The surroundings were suggestive, and after supper they agreed to tell robber stories in turn. "Once there was a [tax collector]." Saying nothing more, he was encouraged to continue. "That," he said, "is the story."
> **— Ambrose Bierce**

romance
noun

1. Fiction that owes no allegiance to reality.

> I so enjoy seeing young lovers smooching in public. Not only does it fill the heart with warm and sentimental feelings, but I'm comforted in the knowledge that the ship of their affections will soon sink on

the rock shores of reality, or sucked forever downward in the maelstrom of marriage.

— **Guy Smith**

Some people claim that marriage interferes with romance. There's no doubt about it. Anytime you have a romance, your wife is bound to interfere.

— **Groucho Marx**

rope
noun

1. An obsolete appliance for reminding assassins that they too are mortal.

[Rope] is put about the neck and remains in place one's whole life long. It has been largely superseded by a more complex electrical device worn upon another part of the person; and this is rapidly giving place to an apparatus known as "parole".

— **Ambrose Bierce [updated by Guy Smith]**

rostrum
noun

1. A place from which a candidate for office energetically expounds the wisdom, virtue, and power of the rabble.

rubbish
noun

1. Worthless matter, such as the religions, philosophies, literatures, arts, and sciences of the tribes infesting the regions lying due south of Scotland.

ruin
verb

1. To destroy a virgin's belief in the virtue of virgins.

There are three paths to ruin – gambling, women and technology. Gambling is the quickest, women are the most enjoyable, but technology is the most reliable.

— **Unknown**

rum
noun

1. Fiery liquors that produce madness in abstainers.

rumor
noun

1. A favorite weapon of the assassins of character.

A rumor without a leg to stand on will get around some other way.
— **John Tudor**

Russian
noun

1. A person with a Caucasian body and a Mongolian soul.

S (AS IN "SUSPICIOUS")

Sabbath
noun

1. A weekly festival having its origin in the fact that God made the world in six days and was arrested on the seventh for violating environmental protection laws.

sacrament
noun

1. A solemn religious ceremony such as the eating of chocolate.

> Rome has seven sacraments, but the Protestant churches, being less prosperous, feel that they can afford only two, and these of inferior sanctity. Some of the smaller sects have no sacraments at all – for which mean economy they will indubitable be damned.
> — **Ambrose Bierce**

sacred
adjective

1. Dedicated to some spiritual purpose or having a spiritual character; the Dalai Lama of Tibet or the Hair of the Dog that Bit You (the latter being a saint of repentance).

sacrifice
noun

1. A form of involuntary penance practiced by the medieval pious.

saint
noun

1. A dead sinner revised and edited.

salamander
noun

1. In America, a lizard. In England, slang for a woman. A graphic description of English women.

San Francisco
noun

1. Hollywood pretending to be New York.

> I was married once – in San Francisco. I haven't seen her for many years. The great earthquake and fire in 1906 destroyed the marriage certificate. There's no legal proof. Which proves that earthquakes aren't all bad.
> — **W.C. Fields**

Satan
noun

1. Standard Bearer of the American Socialist Party.

> And God said "Let there be Satan, so people don't blame everything on me. And let there be lawyers, so people don't blame everything on Satan."
> — **Unknown**

satiety
noun

1. Sexual post-mortem.
2. The feeling that one has for a plate after he has eaten its contents.

satire
noun

1. A kind of literary composition in which the vices and follies of the author's enemies are expounded with imperfect tenderness.

> You can't make up anything anymore. The world itself is a satire. All you're doing is recording it.
>
> **— Art Buchwald**

satirist
noun

1. A person who discovers unpleasant things about himself and then says them about other people.

satyr
noun

1. A creature of Greek mythology made of equal parts man, goat, and testosterone.

> It has been reported that a satyr recently came to America and sought to find Bill Clinton, apparently to acquire an autograph.
>
> **— Guy Smith**

sauce
noun

1. A fairly reliable sign of civilization and enlightenment. This model does not work well in France despite their many sauces.

saw
noun

1. A trite popular saying, or proverb, so called because it makes its way into a woodenhead.

scandal
noun

1. Gossip amplified by morality.

scepter
noun

1. A monarch's weapon of authority.

[The scepter] was originally a mace with which the sovereign admonished his jester and vetoed ministerial measures by breaking the bones of their proponents.

— **Ambrose Bierce**

school
noun

1. The snooze button on the radio clock of life.

In the first place, God made idiots. That was for practice. Then he made school boards.

— **Mark Twain**

science
noun

1. The slaying of a beautiful hypothesis by an ugly fact

Science is like sex: sometimes something useful comes out of it, but that is not the reason we are doing it.

— **Unknown**

The cloning of humans is on most of the lists of things to worry about from Science, along with behavior control, genetic engineering, transplanted heads, computer poetry and the unrestrained growth of plastic flowers.

— **Lewis Thomas**

Science has proof without any certainty. Creationists have certainty without any proof.

— **Ashley Montague**

As an adolescent I aspired to lasting fame, I craved factual certainty, and I thirsted for a meaningful vision of human life - so I became a scientist. This is like becoming an archbishop so you can meet girls.

— **M. Cartmill**

Formerly, when religion was strong and science weak, men mistook magic for medicine; now, when science is strong and religion weak, men mistake medicine for magic.

— **Thomas Szasz**

scrapbook
noun

1. A book with a fool for an author and editor.

scribbler
noun

1. A professional writer whose views are antagonistic to one's own.

scriptures
noun

1. The sacred books of your holy religion, as distinguished from the false and profane books on which all other faiths are based.

secret
noun

1. Something you tell to one person at a time.

> Three may keep a secret, if two of them are dead.
> — **Benjamin Franklin**

seine
noun

1. A kind of net for effecting an involuntary change of environment. For fish, it is made strong and coarse, but women are more easily taken with a loop of gold weighted with small, cut stones.

self-employed
adjective

1. A person who has come to the attention of the Human Resources department for having a large pension entitlement and being close to age fifty.

self-esteem
noun

1. An erroneous appraisement.

self-evident
adjective

1. Evident to one's self and to nobody else.

selfish
adjective

1. Devoid of consideration for the selfishness of others.

2. Singularly concerned with the benefit of the one reliable person in your life.

> To be stupid, selfish, and have good health are three requirements for happiness, though if stupidity is lacking, all is lost.
> — **Gustave Flaubert**

senate
noun

1. An elected governmental body charged with high duties and misdemeanors.

> When they call the roll in the Senate, the Senators do not know whether to answer "Present" or "Not guilty."
> — **Theodore Roosevelt**

serial
noun

1. A literary work creeping through several issues of a newspaper or magazine. Frequently appended to each instalment is a "synopsis of preceding chapters" for those who have not read them, but a direr need is a synopsis of succeeding chapters for those who do not intend to read them. A synopsis of the entire work would be still better.

2. In data communication, the longest chronological distance between point-to-point.

3. In a sequential order such as campaign, election, impeachment, and speaking tour.

seriousness
adjective

1. Refuge of the shallow.

---

sex
noun

1. Biological plumbing differentiating one gender from another, except in San Francisco where such differentiation is considered irrelevant, immoral, and unconstitutional.
2. The natural, and occasionally unnatural, physical union of two or more plants or animals, for the purpose of procreation, sport, or obtaining a husband.
3. The world's favorite participant sport.

> Physics is like sex: sure, it may give some practical results, but that's not why we do it.
> — **Richard P. Feynman.**

> Love is a matter of chemistry, but sex is a matter of physics.
> — **Unknown**

> The best way to get over somebody is to get under somebody.
> — **Lori LaPerle**

> Politics is my second favorite contact sport, right after sex. With either, I know I'm getting screwed.
> — **Guy Smith**

> Alcohol – Helping ugly people have sex since 4,000 B.C.
> — **Bathroom Graffiti**

> Sex is one of the most beautiful, wholesome, and natural things that money can buy.
> — **Steve Martin**

> Children are God's punishment for having sex. And Grandchildren are God's reward for putting up with them.
> — **Ronald Appel**

> Women need a reason to have sex. Men just need a place.
> — **Billy Crystal**

An intellectual is a person who has discovered something more interesting than sex. [Editor: Thank God I'm not an intellectual!]
— Aldous Huxley

Golf and sex are about the only things you can enjoy without being good at.
— Jimmy Demaret

I can remember when the air was clean and sex was dirty.
— George Burns

I know nothing about sex because I was always married.
— Zsa Zsa Gabor

God invented sex and we give praise to him at every orgasm by shouting "Oh, my God."
— Guy Smith

If sex is original sin, Murphyisms are original cynicism.
— Guy Smith

How can sex be "original sin" when humans appeared to being doing little else for millions of years. Doesn't sound very original at all.
— Guy Smith

sheriff
noun

1. In America, the chief law enforcement officer of a country, whose most characteristic duty is fining people for traveling at expedient velocity.

shotgun wedding
noun

1. A case of wife or death.

shyster
noun

1. A crooked, conniving lawyer.
2. Any lawyer.

sin
noun

1. The central pursuit in life, and the major obstacle of the afterlife.

When it comes to finances, there are no withholding taxes on the wages of sin.

— **Mae West**

The wages of sin are unreported.

— **Unknown**

The wages of sin is death, but so is the salary of virtue.

— **Unknown**

The wages of sin are death, but by the time taxes are taken out, it's just sort of a tired feeling.

— **Paula Poundstone**

The world's as ugly as sin, and almost as delightful.

— **Frederick Locker-Lampson**

Women keep a special corner of their hearts for sins they have never committed.

— **Cornelia Otis Skinner**

siren
noun

1. Any lady of splendid promise, dissembled purpose, and disappointing performance.

skeleton
noun

1. Bones with the person scraped off.

slang
noun

1. A means of building a column of wit without a capital of sense.
2. The speech of one who utters with his tongue what he thinks with his ear, and feels the pride of a creator in accomplishing the feat of a parrot.
3. The grunt of the human hog.

Slang is a deliberate invention by professional smart-alecks, college boys, reporters, newspaper men, and other dubious characters.

— **H.L. Mencken**

sleep
noun

1. Death rehearsal.

> Sleep is a totally inadequate substitute for caffeine.
> — **Unknown**

> People who say they sleep like a baby usually don't have one.
> — **Leo J. Burke**

> To achieve the impossible dream, try going to sleep.
> — **Joan Klempner**

> Under even ideal conditions, people have trouble locating their car keys in their pocket, finding their cell phone or playing Pin the Tail on the Donkey. Yet everyone can instantly find and push the snooze button from three feet away, eyes closed, first time, every time.
> — **Unknown**

software
noun

1. A magic spell cast over a computer allowing it to turn one's input into error messages.

> Programming today is a race between software engineers striving to build bigger and better idiot-proof programs, and the Universe trying to produce bigger and better idiots. So far, the Universe is winning.
> — **Rich Cook**

> Software and cathedrals are much the same – first we build them, then we pray.
> — **Unknown**

sorcery
noun

1. The ancient prototype and forerunner of political influence.

soul
noun

1. That fundamental, spiritual essence of humans - their direct connection to God - that is readily purchasable.
2. A musical genre devoid of its namesake.

> Hollywood is a place where they'll pay you a thousand dollars for a kiss and fifty cents for your soul.
> — **Marilyn Monroe**

statistician
noun

1. A man who believes figures don't lie, but admits that under analysis some of them won't stand up either.

statistics
noun

1. The only science that enables different experts using the same figures to draw different conclusions.

> A single death is a tragedy; a million deaths is a statistic.
> — **Joseph Stalin**

> Facts are stubborn things, but statistics are more pliable.
> — **Laurence J. Peter**

> Smoking is one of the leading causes of statistics.
> — **Fletcher Knebel**

> There are three kinds of lies: lies, damned lies, and statistics.
> — **Benjamin Disraeli**

> 73.6% of statistics are made up on the spot!
> — **Unknown**

stock split
noun

1. When your ex-wife and her lawyer split all your assets equally between themselves.

story

noun

1. A narrative, commonly untrue, most commonly a State of the Union address or Quarterly SEC filing.

Bad decisions make for good stories.
— **Unknown**

stubbornness

adjective

1. Always knowing what you will be thinking tomorrow.

stupidity

noun

1. The true measure of equality across all races, creeds, genders, sexuality and social status.

Strange as it seems, no amount of learning can cure stupidity, and formal education positively fortifies it.
— **Stephen Vizinczey**

There is no nonsense so gross that society will not, at some time, make a doctrine of it and defend it with every weapon of communal stupidity.
— **Robertson Davies**

With stupidity the gods themselves contend in vain.
— **Friedrich von Schiller**

The two most abundant elements in the universe are Hydrogen and stupidity.
— **Harlan Ellison**

Never attribute to malice what can be adequately explained by stupidity.
— **Nick Diamos**

Genius may have its limitations, but stupidity is not thus handicapped.
— **Elbert Hubbard**

Artificial Intelligence is no match for natural stupidity.

— **Unknown**

Only two things are infinite, the universe and human stupidity, and I'm not sure about the former.

— **Albert Einstein**

Never underestimate the power of human stupidity.

— **Robert Heinlein**

In democracy, stupidity always holds the majority in every chamber of government. It is, after all, a representative system.

— **William Ferraiolo**

subversive
noun

1. Anyone who can out-argue their government.

success
noun

1. Attendance plus luck.
2. An unpardonable sin against one's neighbors.

Nothing changes your opinion of a friend so surely as success – yours or his.

— **Franklin P. Jones**

Each success only buys an admission ticket to a more difficult problem.

— **Henry Kissinger**

Nothing succeeds like the appearance of success.

— **Christopher Lasch**

To succeed in the world it is not enough to be stupid, you must also be well-mannered.

— **Voltaire**

Since government rarely succeeds, it hardly ever fails.

— **P.J. O'Rourke**

If at first you don't succeed, well, so much for skydiving.

— **Victor O'Reilly**

Success and failure are both difficult to endure. Along with success come drugs, divorce, fornication, bullying, travel, meditation, medication, depression, neurosis and suicide. With failure comes failure.
— **Joseph Heller**

There's no secret about success. Did you ever know a successful man who didn't tell you about it?
— **Kin Hubbard**

The world tolerates conceit from those who are successful, but not from anybody else.
— **John Blake**

If at first don't succeed, find out if the loser gets anything.
— **Bill Lyon**

The penalty for success is to be bored by the people who used to snub you.
— **Nancy Astor**

The secret of success is sincerity. Once you can fake that you've got it made.
— **Jean Giraudoux**

All you need in this life is ignorance and confidence, and then success is sure.
— **Mark Twain**

We must believe in luck. For how else can we explain the success of those we don't like?
— **Jean Cocteau**

Behind every successful man stands a surprised mother-in-law.
— **Hubert H. Humphrey**

suffrage
noun

1. Expression of self-delusion by means of a ballot.

The right of suffrage (which is held to be both a privilege and a duty) means, as commonly interpreted, the right to vote for the man of another man's choice, and is highly prized. Refusal to do so has the bad name of "incivism." The incivilian, however, cannot be properly arraigned for his crime, for there is no legitimate accuser. If the accuser is himself guilty he has no standing in the court of opinion; if not, he profits by the crime, for A's abstention from voting gives greater weight to the vote of B.

— **Ambrose Bierce**

suicide
noun

1. Your way of telling God "You can't fire me! I quit!"
2. The most sincere form of self-criticism.

There are many who dare not kill themselves for fear of what the neighbors will say.

— **Cyril Connolly**

sycophant
noun

1. One who approaches Greatness on his belly so that he cannot be commanded to turn and be kicked (see *literary agent*)

syllogism
noun

1. A logical formula consisting of a major and a minor assumption, and an inconsequent.

synonym
noun

1. A word you use when you can't spell the word you first thought of.

 (AS IN "TRENCHANT")

tact
noun

1. The ability to describe others as they see themselves.

tail
noun

1. The extended portion of a dog's spine equipped with an independently operating motor, not to be confused with a similar apparatus found on men who are also referred to as dogs.

take
transitive verb

1. To acquire, frequently by force but preferably by stealth (see *taxation*).

> He who praises you for what you lack wishes to take from you what you have.
> — **Don Juan Manuel**

talk
noun

1. An exchange of ideas, opinions, disagreements, threats, declarations of war, ultimatums, terms of surrender, or peace accords. Rewind and repeat.

transitive verb

2. The process used by humans to modulate sounds produced from the mouth for the purpose of miscommunication.

> Talk is cheap ... except when Congress speaks.
> — **Unknown**

Great people talk about ideas, average people talk about things, and small people talk about wine.
— **Fran Lebowitz**

The prime purpose of eloquence is to keep other people from talking.
— **Louis Vermeil**

You never see a fish on the wall with its mouth shut.
— **Unknown**

It is a common delusion that you make things better by talking about them.
— **Dame Rose Macaulay**

God burdened man with multiple languages to slow our progress, for only God knows how really ^%(&#* dangerous we are.
— **Guy Smith**

Saying what we think gives us a wider conversational range than saying what we know.
— **Cullen Hightower**

tariff
noun

1. A tax on imports, designed to protect the domestic producer against the greed of his consumer.

taxpayer
noun

1. Someone who works for the government but doesn't have to take a civil service exam.

I'm proud to be paying taxes in the United States. The only thing is I could be just as proud for half the money.
— **Arthur Godfrey**

technicality
noun

1. law: the product procured by criminals from other criminals, specifically lawyers.
2. The nit picked by shaven apes.

technology

noun

1. A way of organizing the universe so that man doesn't have to experience it.

> Always be wary of any helpful item that weighs less than its operating manual.
> — **Terry Pratchett**

> The marvels of modern technology include the development of a soda can which, when discarded, will last forever and a $7,000 car, which, when properly cared for, will rust out in two or three years.
> — **Paul Harwitz**

> There are three paths to ruin – gambling, women and technology. Gambling is the quickest, women are the most enjoyable, but technology is the most reliable.
> — **Unknown**

> For a list of all the ways technology has failed to improve the quality of life, please press three.
> — **Alice Kahn**

tedium

noun

1. Ennui, the state or condition of one that is gainfully employed.

teetotaler

noun

1. One who abstains from strong drink, sometimes totally, sometimes tolerably.

telephone

noun

1. A device for extending miscommunications great distances. The absence of face-to-face interaction amplifies the effects.
2. An invention whose chief purpose is to make a disagreeable person keep his distance.

The Americans have need of the telephone, but we do not. We have plenty of messenger boys.
— **Sir William Preece, chief engineer of the British Post Office, 1876**

telescope
noun

1. A device enabling distant objects to plague us with a multitude of needless details.

television
noun

1. Chewing gum for the eyes.
2. A modern alter upon which intelligence is sacrificed.

Television is simultaneously blamed, often by the same people, for worsening the world and for being powerless to change it.
— **Clive James**

Television has made dictatorship impossible but democracy unbearable.
— **Shimon Peres**

Television has changed the American child from in irresistible force into an immovable object.
— **Unknown**

Of what you see in books, believe 75%. Of newspapers, believe 25%. And of TV news, believe 10% – make that 5% if the anchorman wears a blazer.
— **Unknown**

Television is the first truly democratic culture – the first culture available to everybody and entirely governed by what the people want. The most terrifying thing is what people do want.
— **Clive Barnes**

Why watch reality TV in a TV based reality?
— **RayB**

Television news is like a lightning flash. It makes a loud noise, lights up everything around it, leaves everything else in darkness and then is suddenly gone.
— **Hodding Carter**

Television has proved that people will look at anything rather than each other.

— **Ann Landers**

Imitation is the sincerest form of television.

— **Fred Allen**

CNN is one of the participants in the war. I have a fantasy where Ted Turner is elected president but refuses because he doesn't want to give up power.

— **Arthur C. Clarke**

Television has raised writing to a new low.

— **Samuel Goldwyn**

All television is children's television.

— **Richard P. Adler**

Seeing a murder on television ... can help work off one's antagonisms. And if you haven't any antagonisms, the commercials will give you some.

— **Alfred Hitchcock**

Television has done much for psychiatry by spreading information about it, as well as contributing to the need for it.

— **Alfred Hitchcock**

The human race is faced with a cruel choice: work or daytime television.

— **Unknown**

Television – a medium. So called because it is neither rare nor well done.

— **Ernie Kovacs**

Television enables you to be entertained in your home by people you wouldn't have in your home.

— **David Frost**

When the politicians complain that TV turns the proceedings into a circus, it should be made clear that the circus was already there, and that TV has merely demonstrated that not all the performers are well trained.

— **Edward R. Murrow**

Don't you wish there were a knob on the TV to turn up the intelligence? There's one marked "brightness," but it doesn't work.

— **Gallagher**

It's hard to decide if TV makes morons out of everyone or if it mirrors Americans who really are morons to begin with.
— **Martin Mull**

tenacity
noun

1. A certain quality of the human hand in its relation to money. It attains its highest development in the hand of government and is considered serviceable equipment for a career in politics.

terrorist
noun

1. Political activists skilled at the art of persuasion through explosives.

We should not be surprised that the abbreviation of the names of two of the most despised terrorist groups are so similar, they being the IRA and the IRS.
— **Guy Smith**

think
verb

1. The rearranging of prejudices.

Anyone who has begun to think places some portion of the world in jeopardy.
— **John Dewey**

Aristotle believed that the brain existed merely to cool blood and was not involved in with thinking, which has proven true for certain persons, mainly politicians.
— **Derived from Will Cuppy**

A bookstore is one of the only pieces of evidence we have that people are still thinking.
— **Jerry Seinfeld**

I work in a think tank in which I am free to say what they pay me to say.
— **Sok Sombong**

If you make people think they're thinking, they'll love you; But if you really make them think, they'll hate you.

— **Don Marquis**

The world is a tragedy to those who feel, but a comedy to those who think.

— **Horace Walpole**

Ours is the age that is proud of machines that think and suspicious of men who try to.

— **H. Mumford Jones**

It is not a bad idea to get in the habit of writing down one's thoughts. It saves one having to bother anyone else with them.

— **Isabel Colegate**

Never express yourself more clearly than you are able to think.

— **Niels Bohr**

Many people would sooner die than think; In fact, they do so.

— **Bertrand Russell**

If two men agree on everything, you may be sure that one of them is doing the thinking.

— **Lyndon B. Johnson**

There is no expedient to which a man will not go to avoid the labor of thinking.

— **Thomas A. Edison**

Don't worry about what people think; they don't do it very often.

— **Unknown**

Saying what we think gives us a wider conversational range than saying what we know.

— **Cullen Hightower**

Men and women both think like spaghetti. Men's mental spaghetti is uncooked and runs in straight lines. Women's is well boiled and point in every direction simultaneously.

— **Ralph Seifert**

tomb

noun

1. The House of Permanent Indifference.

tomorrow
noun

1. One of the greatest labor saving devices of today.

tope
verb

1. To tipple, booze, swill, soak, guzzle, lush, bib, swig, or in some other way enjoy life.

> In the individual, toping is regarded with disesteem, but toping nations are in the forefront of civilization and power. When pitted against the hard-drinking Christians the abstemious Mahometans go down like grass before the scythe. In India one hundred thousand beef-eating and brandy-and-soda guzzling Britons hold in subjection two hundred and fifty million vegetarian abstainers of the same Aryan race. With what an easy grace the whisky-loving American pushed the temperate Spaniard out of his possessions! From the time when the Berserkers ravaged all the coasts of Western Europe and lay drunk in every conquered port it has been the same way: everywhere the nations that drink too much are observed to fight rather well and not too righteously. Wherefore the estimable old ladies who abolished the canteen from the American army may justly boast of having materially augmented the nation's military power.
> — **Ambrose Bierce**

tradition

1. Group efforts to keep unexpected things from happening.

> Tradition is what you resort to when you don't have the time or the money to do it right.
> — **Kurt Herbert Alder**

tragedy
noun

1. The ills you wish upon your enemy that fall upon yourself.

> A single death is a tragedy; a million deaths is a statistic.
> — **Joseph Stalin**

> The world is a tragedy to those who feel, but a comedy to those who think.
> — **Horace Walpole**

> Tragedy is when I cut my finger. Comedy is when you walk into an open sewer and die.
> — **Mel Brooks**

trailer
noun

1. Tornado food.

tree
noun

1. A tall vegetable intended by nature to serve as a penal apparatus.

trial
noun

1. A formal inquiry designed to prove the blameless characters of judges, advocates, and jurors.

> In order to effect this purpose it is necessary to supply a contrast in the person of one who is called the defendant, the prisoner, or the accused. If the contrast is made sufficiently clear this person is made to undergo such an affliction as will give the virtuous gentlemen a comfortable sense of their immunity, added to that of their worth. In our day the accused is usually a human being, or a socialist.
> — **Ambrose Bierce**

trichinosis
noun

1. The pig's reply to proponents of "the other white meat" advertising campaign.

trinity
noun

1. Original schizophrenia.

2. In certain Christian churches, three entirely distinct deities resident in one distinct being.

> The Trinity is one of the most sublime mysteries of our holy religion. In rejecting it because it is incomprehensible, Unitarians betray their inadequate sense of theological fundamentals. In religion we believe only what we do not understand, except in the instance of an intelligible doctrine that contradicts an incomprehensible one. In that case we believe the former as a part of the latter.
> — **Ambrose Bierce**

troglodyte
noun

1. One of mankind's predecessors placed chronologically before Luddites but after socialists.

truce
noun

1. Friendship.
2. A formal declaration of peace between warring nations or individuals for the express purpose of rearming.

trust
noun

1. law: a legal document or entity in which the lawyer steals from his client.
2. business: a corporation designed for performing untrustworthy acts.
3. The landmine of indecision.
4. politics: a constituency composed mainly of thrifty working men, widows of small means, orphans in the care of guardians and the courts, with many similar malefactors and public enemies.

> The people I distrust most are those who want to improve our lives but have only one course of action.
> — **Frank Herbert**

> Nobody believes the official spokesman ... but everybody trusts an unidentified source.

— **Ron Nesen**

Lawyers make ample use of the word "trust" while instilling in everyone they meet a complete lack thereof.

— **Guy Smith**

truth

noun

1. An ingenious compound of desirability and appearance.
2. Well-aged blasphemies.

Chase after truth like hell and you'll free yourself, even though you never touch its coat-tails.

— **Clarence Darrow**

They shall not overcome. Whoever told them that the truth shall set them free was obviously and grossly unfamiliar with federal law.

— **John Ashcroft**

Most people, sometime in their lives, stumble across truth. And most jump up, brush themselves off, and hurry on about their business as if nothing had happened.

— **Winston Churchill**

All truth passes through three stages. First, it is ridiculed. Second, it is violently opposed. Third, it is accepted as being self-evident.

— **Arthur Schopenhauer**

The truth that makes men free is for the most part the truth which men prefer not to hear.

— **Herbert Agar**

Autobiography is an unrivaled vehicle for telling the truth about other people.

— **Philip Guedalla**

There are only two ways of telling the complete truth – anonymously and posthumously.

— **Thomas Sowell**

A lie can travel halfway around the world while the truth is putting on its shoes.

— **Mark Twain**

It is hard to believe that a man is telling the truth when you know that you would lie if you were in his place.
— **H.L. Mencken**

Speak the truth, but leave immediately after.
— **Unknown**

The public will believe anything, so long as it is not founded on truth.
— **Edith Sitwell**

It is amazing the number of people who are pleased by the simple act of sincerely professing the truth. I mean, I would have thought there would have been at least one.
— **John Alejandro King**

It is always the best policy to speak the truth – unless, of course, you are an exceptionally good liar.
— **Jerome K. Jerome**

If a man speaks of his honor, make him pay cash.
— **Robert Heinlein**

The truth is rarely pure and never simple.
— **Oscar Wilde**

A politician under oath is a bit like a tumor under chemotherapy.
— **William Ferraiolo**

Believe those who are seeking the truth. Doubt those who find it.
— **Andre Gide**

truthful
adjective

1. Dumb and illiterate.

turkey
noun

1. A large bird whose flesh, when eaten on certain religious anniversaries, has the peculiar property of attesting piety and gratitude.

turtle
noun

1. A creature created to be fast and agile when compared to a government bureaucrat.

 (AS IN "UNDECEIVED")

ubiquity
noun

1. The annoying power of being in all places at one time, possessed by God, mosquitoes and people of low intelligence.

ugliness
noun

1. A gift from God to certain people, providing them virtue without humility.

> Here is something that the psychologists have so far neglected: the love of ugliness for its own sake, the lust to make the world intolerable. Its habitat is the United States.
> **— H.L. Mencken**

ultimatum
noun

1. The ultimate show of love and trust as practiced in America.
2. In diplomacy, a last demand before resorting to concessions.

Un-American
adjective

1. Of, or having any of, the political sensibilities of fascism, socialism, communism, or any other two-bit regime established by American foreign policy.

understanding
noun

1. The mental process of misperceiving your reality better than your neighbor misperceives his.

Unitarian
noun

1. One who denies the divinity of a Trinitarian.

Universalist
noun

1. One who forgoes the advantages of Hell for persons of another faith.

university
noun

1. A college after the faculty loses interest in students.

> University politics are vicious precisely because the stakes are so small.
> **— Henry Kissinger**
>
> A fool's brain digests philosophy into folly, science into superstition, and art into pedantry. Hence University education.
> **— George Bernard Shaw**

Unix
noun

1. A computer operating system, once thought to be flabby and impotent, that now shows a surprising interest in making off with the computer harem.

unmentionables
noun

1. Articles of ladies' apparel that are never discussed in public, except in full-page, illustrated ads.

urbanity
noun

1. A kind of civility that observers ascribe to dwellers in all cities except New York.

 (AS IN "VENOMOUS")

valor
noun

1. A compound mixed by soldiers, composed of equal measures of vanity, duty, and the gambler's hope.

value investing
noun

1. The art of buying low and selling lower.

vanity
noun

1. Tributes made by fools to the worth of the nearest ass.

vice
noun

1. Activities that make life worth living.

> It has been my experience that folks who have no vices have very few virtues.
> — **Abraham Lincoln**

> Good taste is the worst vice ever invented.
> — **Edith Sitwell**

> The problem with people who have no vices is that generally you can be pretty sure they're going to have some pretty annoying virtues.
> — **Elizabeth Taylor**

virtue
noun

1. Primary personality trait and implement for annoying others.
2. Its own punishment.

The wages of sin is death, but so is the salary of virtue.
— **Unknown**

No one gossips about other people's secret virtues.
— **Bertrand Russell**

The virtues we attribute to people at their best – loyalty and devotion, courage and gentleness, integrity and spirit – are found so rarely that we name schools for the men and women who display them. But you'd be hard pressed to find a dog who doesn't live them every day.
— **Scott Raab**

virtues
noun

1. Certain regrettable abstentions.

vote
noun

1. The art of choosing between the disastrous and the unpalatable.

2. The instrument and symbol of a freeman's power to make a fool of himself and a wreck of his country.

3. The common currency of organized insurrection.

4. The chief tool used by politicians to pick the pockets of the populace and make citizens thank them for the privilege.

The problem with political jokes is they get elected.
— **Henry Cate VII**

The difference between a democracy and a dictatorship is that in a democracy you vote first and take orders later; in a dictatorship you don't have to waste your time voting.
— **Charles Bukowski**

It doesn't matter who you vote for ... the government always gets in.
— **Unknown**

A citizen of America will cross the ocean to fight for democracy, but won't cross the street to vote in a national election.
— **Bill Vaughan**

There may be no candidates and measures you want to vote for ... But there are certain to be ones you want to vote against. In case of doubt, vote against. By this rule you will rarely go wrong.

If this is too blind for your taste, consult some well-meaning fool (there is always one around) and ask his advice. Then vote the other way. This enables you to be a good citizen (if such is your wish) without spending the enormous amount of time that truly intelligent exercise of the franchise requires.

— **Robert Heinlein**

Half of the American people have never read a newspaper. Half never voted for President. One hopes it is the same half.

— **Gore Vidal**

voter
noun

1. A person who every election cycle dutifully deceives themselves into believing his vote counts.

Nothing can so alienate a voter from the political system as backing a winning candidate.

— **Mark B. Cohen**

 (AS IN "WISEASS")

Wall Street
noun

1. A symbol of sin for failed thieves.
2. The world's largest gambling casino.

war
noun

1. A process by which it is legal to steal from someone else, and in doing so usually spend far more than the potential gain.
2. A by-product of the arts of peace.
3. Proof that violence does solve things.
4. The mass reallocation of resources from one nation to another.

War is like love; it always finds a way.
— **Unknown**

Take the diplomacy out of war and the thing would fall flat in a week.
— **Will Rogers**

The only winner in the War of 1812 was Tchaikovsky.
— **Solomon Short**

How is it possible to have a civil war?
— **Unknown**

War is a series of catastrophes that results in a victory.
— **Georges Clemenceau**

It is well that war is so terrible, or we should grow too fond of it.
— **Robert E. Lee**

Wars teach us not to love our enemies, but to hate our allies.
— **W.L. George**

The most menacing political condition is a period of international amity. The student of history who has not been taught to expect the unexpected may justly boast himself inaccessible to the light. "In time of peace prepare for war" has a deeper meaning than is commonly discerned; it means, not merely that all things earthly have an end – that change is the one immutable and eternal law – but that the soil of peace is thickly sown with the seeds of war and singularly suited to their germination and growth.

— Ambrose Bierce

"What if we had a war and nobody came?" Then marketing did a lousy job of promoting the event.

— Unknown

warhead
noun

1. The final arbiter in international disputes.

Washingtonian
noun

1. A Potomac tribesman who exchanged the privilege of governing himself for the disadvantage of good government.

weaknesses
noun

1. Certain primal powers of woman wherewith they hold dominion over the male of her species, binding him to the service of her will and paralyzing his rebellious energies.

People who have no weaknesses are terrible; there is no way of taking advantage of them.

— Anatole France

weather
noun

1. The climate of the hour.

The trouble with weather forecasting is that it's right too often for us to ignore it and wrong too often for us to rely on it.

— Patrick Young

Don't knock the weather. If it didn't change once in a while, nine out of ten people couldn't start a conversation.

— **Kin Hubbard**

[Weather is a] permanent topic of conversation among persons whom it does not interest, but who have inherited the tendency to chatter about it from naked arboreal ancestors whom it keenly concerned. The setting up official weather bureaus and their maintenance in mendacity prove that even governments are accessible to suasion by the rude forefathers of the jungle.

— **Ambrose Bierce**

Isn't it interesting that the same people who laugh at science fiction listen to weather forecasts and economists?

— **Kelvin Throop III**

wedding
noun

1. A paradoxical event often mistaken as a birth (by the bride) and a funeral (by the groom).

2. A funeral where you smell your own flowers.

3. A ceremony at which two persons undertake to become one, one undertakes to become nothing, and nothing is undertaken to become supportable.

The only difference between a wedding and a funeral is there is one less person standing at a funeral.

— **Cliff Cole**

werewolf
noun

1. A wolf that was once, or is sometimes, a man and who is as humane and consistent with their acquired taste for human flesh.

wheat
noun

1. A cereal from which a tolerably good whisky can with some difficulty be made, and which is used also for bread.

The French are said to eat more bread per capita of population than any other people, which is natural, for only they know how to make the stuff palatable [Editor: and because the French have such picky palates that only they could tolerate such a diet].
— **Ambrose Bierce**

whiskey
noun

1. A drink of heroes because only heroes would dare drink the stuff.
2. A consumable liquid made of one part thunder-and-lighting, one part remorse, two parts bloody murder, one part death-hell-and-grave, and four parts Satan (all of which explains its raging popularity).

widow
noun

1. A woman prematurely liberated from marriage without the negative stigma associated with other methods.
2. A married woman whose husband is taking an extended nap.

All work and no play makes Jack a dull boy and Jill a rich widow.
— **Evan Esar**

There is only one way to console a widow. But remember the risk.
— **Robert Heinlein**

wife
noun

1. Your bitter half.

One good husband is worth two good wives; for the scarcer things are, the more they are valued.
— **Benjamin Franklin**

Man and wife make one fool.
— **Ben Jonson**

By all means marry; if you get a good wife, you'll be happy. If you get a bad one, you'll become a philosopher.
— **Socrates**

One man's folly is another man's wife.

> — Helen Rowland

> When a man steals your wife, there is no better revenge than to let him keep her.
>
> — King David

> I had some words with my wife, and she had some paragraphs with me.
>
> — Sigmund Freud

willy-nilly
adjective

1. Impotent.

wine
noun

1. 1/10 of man's nutrition and 9/10 of his good humor.

2. Fermented grape-juice known to the Temperance Union as "liquor".

> Great people talk about ideas, average people talk about things, and small people talk about wine.
>
> — Fran Lebowitz

> Wine makes a man more pleased with himself; I do not say that it makes him more pleasing to others.
>
> — Samuel Johnson

wisdom
noun

1. What remains after depleting personal opinions.

> Intelligence is when you spot a flaw in your boss's reasoning. Wisdom is when you refrain from pointing it out.
>
> — James Dent

> Wisdom is knowing what to do next; virtue is doing it.
>
> — David Starr Jordan

> Just because your voice reaches halfway around the world doesn't mean you are wiser than when it reached only to the end of the bar.
>
> — Edward R. Murrow

wit
noun

1. The salt with which a humorist spoils his intellectual cookery by leaving it out.

The ability to quote is a serviceable substitute for wit.
— **W. Somerset Maugham**

witch
noun

1. Any ugly and repulsive old woman, in a wicked league with the devil (see *mother-in-law*).
2. A beautiful and attractive young woman, in wickedness a league beyond the devil (see *wife*).

witticism
noun

1. A sharp and clever remark, usually quoted, and seldom cited.

woman
noun

1. A creature so overwhelmed by sensitivity that they are rendered senseless.
2. An animal usually living in the vicinity of man, and having a rudimentary susceptibility to domestication.

From birth to 18 a girl needs good parents. From 18 to 35, she needs good looks. From 35 to 55, good personality. From 55 on, she needs good cash.
— **Sophie Tucker**

A woman can fake an orgasm, but it takes a man to fake an entire relationship.
— **Unknown**

In politics, if you want anything said, ask a man – if you want anything done, ask a woman.
— **Margaret Thatcher**

Any woman who thinks the way to a man's heart is through his stomach is aiming about 10 inches too high.

— **Adrienne E. Gusoff**

Every man is wise when attacked by a mad dog; fewer when pursued by a mad woman.

— **Robertson Davies**

Once a woman passes a certain point in intelligence it is almost impossible to get a husband: she simply cannot go on listening [to men] without snickering.

— **H.L. Mencken**

Women are often referred to as the "gentle" sex. I believe this adjective describes the sweetly undetectable method in which women insert a knife in a man's back.

— **Guy Smith**

[Women are] credited by many of the elder zoologists with a certain vestigial docility acquired in a former state of seclusion, but naturalists of the post-susan-anthony period, having no knowledge of the seclusion, deny the virtue and declare that such as creation's dawn beheld, it roareth now. The species is the most widely distributed of all beasts of prey, infesting all habitable parts of the globe, from Greeland's spicy mountains to India's moral strand. The popular name (wolfman) is incorrect, for the creature is of the cat kind. The woman is lithe and graceful in its movement, especially the American variety (felis pugnans), is omnivorous and can be taught not to talk.

— **Ambrose Bierce**

Whatever you give a woman, she's going to multiply. If you give her sperm, she'll give you a baby. If you give her a house, she'll give you a home. If you give her groceries, she'll give you a meal. If you give her a smile, she'll give you her heart. She multiplies and enlarges all that is given to her. So, if you give her any crap, you will receive a ton of s**t.

— **Unknown**

The only way to be truly misogynistic is to be a woman.

— **Randy K. Milholland**

---

world
noun

1. A tragedy to people that feel, a comedy to people that think.

I think the world is run by "C" students.
— Al McGuire

If all the world's a stage, I want to operate the trap door.
— Paul Beatty

The world is round; it has no point.
— Adrienne E. Gusoff

In the fight between you and the world, back the world.
— Frank Zappa

The world's as ugly as sin, and almost as delightful.
— Frederick Locker-Lampson

All the world's a cage.
— Jeanne Phillips

All the world's a stage and most of us are desperately unrehearsed.
— Sean O'Casey

The more you find out about the world, the more opportunities there are to laugh at it.
— Bill Nye

worship
noun

1. A popular form of abjection, having an element of pride.
2. religion: the process of proclaiming one's lack of worth in order to obtain a worthy status.

The more I study religions the more I am convinced that man never worshipped anything but himself.
— Sir Richard Francis Burton

Thousands of years ago, cats were worshipped as gods. Cats have never forgotten this.
— Unknown

wrath
noun

1. Anger of a superior quality and degree, appropriate to exalted characters and momentous occasions.

"Wrath" is most commonly attributed to God and women. This should give men something to fear.

— Guy Smith

writer
noun

1. An author with lower literary expectations and higher gross income.

Many people hear voices when no-one is there. Some of them are called mad and are shut up on rooms where they stare at the walls all day. Others are called writers and they do pretty much the same thing.

— Meg Chittenden

Writers are lunatics, except for the good writers, who are maniacs.

— William H. Macy

About the most originality that any writer can hope to achieve honestly is to steal with good judgment.

— Josh Billings

Asking a working writer what he thinks about critics is like asking a lamppost how it feels about dogs.

— Christopher Hampton

The cure for writer's cramp is writer's block.

— Inigo DeLeon

Some editors are failed writers, but so are most writers.

— T. S. Eliot

I'm all in favor of keeping dangerous weapons out of the hands of fools. Let's start with typewriters.

— Solomon Short

Everywhere I go I'm asked if I think the university stifles writers. My opinion is that they don't stifle enough of them. There's many a best-seller that could have been prevented by a good teacher.

— Flannery O'Connor

Most writers are drunkards and fools. Having lived foolishly for most of my life and having mastered the art of drunkardy, I concluded that I might as well write.

— Charles Gilbert

First you're an unknown, then you write one book and you move up to obscurity.
— **Martin Myers**

WWW
noun

1. World Wide Wait.

Y (AS IN "YIKES")

yawn
noun

1. An honest opinion openly expressed.

year
noun

1. A period of three hundred and sixty-five disappointments.

yesterday
noun

1. The infancy of youth, the youth of manhood, the ancient history of old age.

youth
noun

1. The Period of Possibility, followed by Fortnights of Folly.

> Blessed are the young for they shall inherit the national debt.
> — **Unknown**

> The young always have the same problem – how to rebel and conform at the same time. They have now solved this by defying their parents and copying one another.
> — **George Chapman**

> To get back my youth I would do anything in the world, except take exercise, get up early, or be respectable.
> — **Oscar Wilde**

> The secret of eternal youth is arrested development.
> — **Alice Roosevelt Longworth**

 (AS IN "ZED")

zeal
noun

1. A passion that goeth before a sprawl.
2. A certain nervous disorder afflicting the young and inexperienced.

www.ingramcontent.com/pod-product-compliance
Lightning Source LLC
Chambersburg PA
CBHW022354040426
42450CB00005B/173